Japanese

FOLDED PATCHWORK

Techniques, projects, and designs
of a unique Asian craft

Mary Clare Clark

Dedicated to: Ikuko Obata with thanks.

A QUINTET BOOK

ISBN 0-8019-9046-7

Krause Publications
700 E. State St.
Iola, WI 54990-0001
Telephone: 715-445-2214

Please call or write for our free catalog of publications. Our toll-free number to place an
order or obtain a free catalog is 800-258-0929 or please use our regular business telephone
715-445-2214 for editorial comment and further information.

This book was designed and produced by Quintet Publishing Ltd.

Creative Director: Richard Dewing
Art Director: Silke Braun
Designer: Isobel Gillan
Senior Editor: Anna Briffa
Editor: Samantha Gray
Photographer: Jon Bouchier
Illustrator: Elsa Godfrey
Charts by: Jenny Dooge
Templates by: Joanna Cameron

Typeset in Great Britain by
Central Southern Typesetters, Eastbourne
Manufactured in Singapore by Pica Colour Separation Overseas Pte. Ltd.
Printed in Singapore by Star Standard Industries (Pte.) Ltd.

ACKNOWLEDGEMENTS

◆■◆■◆■◆■◆■◆■◆■◆■◆□◆■◆◆■◆■◆■◆■◆■◆■◆■◆■◆■◆

QUILTMAKER		QUILT
Christine Challen	–	Batik
Corinne Everson	–	Antique Flowers, Circus Cot Quilt, Anemones de Caen
Lynda Guy	–	Wallhanging
Prue Harding	–	Bandanas and Jeans
Tina Lamborn	–	Green Flower Throwover
Myra Shipton	–	Handkerchiefs
Georgia Rodope	–	Hexagon Bag

Contents

Introduction

The Japanese folded patchwork technique was first introduced to me by a Japanese student who had gone home for a visit and found a book on this type of patchwork. The instructions were in Japanese, of course, but they were photographed and illustrated very well.

I thought that I would only have access to the book for two weeks and all the other students wanted to know how the patchwork was done. So I set about making folded shapes of the basic patterns out of wrapping paper, much like origami. I found the technique very versatile and inspiring. We then went on to make variations from the original style.

Because each folded patchwork square is a self-contained unit, it is possible to make them as you go along, during a busy day, watching television, or on holiday. Joining the pieces when you have the time and space almost makes an instant quilt, which is very rewarding. I hope you find these techniques and designs as inspiring and exciting as we all do.

◆■●◆■●◆■●◆■●◆■●◆■●◆■●◆■●◆■●◆■●◆■●◆■●◆■●◆■●◆■●

Squares into Squares

WITH SIMPLE, FOLDED SQUARES, A WIDE VARIETY OF CONTRASTING PATCHES CAN BE MADE. ONCE SEWN TOGETHER THEY CAN GIVE CROSSES AND DIAMOND PATTERNS, CHEVRONS, AND MANY MORE.

PATTERN GUIDES

Cut out paper pattern guides with these squares:

Pattern A: The size of the large squares when cut out

Pattern B: The finished size of the large squares and the cut size for padding

Pattern C: The size of the small squares when cut out

Pattern D: The finished size of the small squares

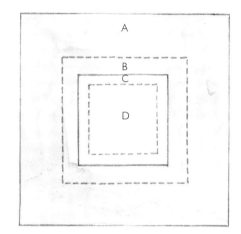

Cut two pieces of fabric using patterns A and C, and one piece of padding using pattern B.

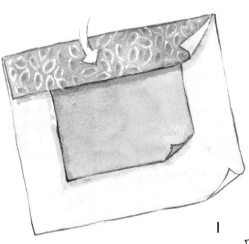

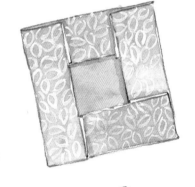

1. Center pattern B on the wrong side of the fabric square cut using pattern A.

2. Fold the edges of the fabric over the pattern and press in place.

3. Remove the pattern, place padding in the square aligning the edges along the crease lines.

4. Miter the corners of the fabric square by folding them into the center and pressing in place.

5. Then refold the sides into the center, aligning the diagonal creases, press and pin in place.

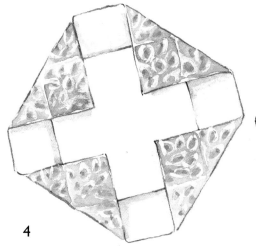

4

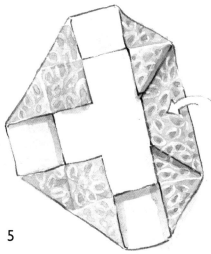

5

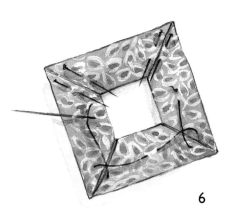

6

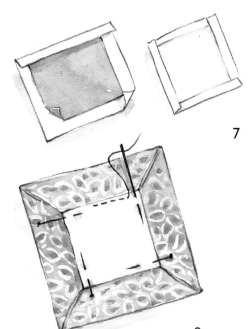

7

8

6. Baste the corners to hold them in place when quilting.

7. Center pattern D on the wrong side of the fabric square cut with pattern C. Fold the edges of the fabric over the pattern and press in place.

8. Remove the pattern and place the small square right side up in the center of the large square. Match the corners with the mitered corners of the large square and pin the corners together. Quilt the pieces together along the inside of the small square. Start to stitch on a side, not on a corner, with the thread end anchored between the layers. Finish in the same way.

VARIATIONS TO SQUARES
◆■◉■◆■◉■◆■◉■◆■◉■◆■◉■◆■◉■◆■◉■◆■◉■◆■◉■◆

The squares can be made of halved or quartered squares to create additional patterns depending upon the order in which they are placed (see *Roman Stripes* p.36 and *Crosses and Diamonds* p.32). They can also be pieced in patchwork blocks, with the sides of the blocks extended, to create a double-sided quilt (see *Windows* and *Victorian Tiles* pp.43–51).

Circles into Squares

◆■●◆■●◆■●◆■●◆■●◆■●◆■●◆■●◆■●◆■●◆■●◆■●◆■●◆■●◆■●◆■●◆■

FOLDING A WHOLE CIRCLE OF ONE FABRIC OVER A SQUARE OF ANOTHER,
CONTRASTING FABRIC, AND ALTERNATING THE COLORS OVER SEVERAL SQUARES
GIVES A FLOWER SHAPE ON THE FRONT AND A CHECKERBOARD DESIGN
ON THE BACK

PATTERN GUIDES

◆■●◆■●◆■●◆■●◆■●◆■●◆■●◆■●◆■◆

Cut out paper pattern guides with these circles and square:

Pattern A: The size of the circles when cut out

Pattern B: The finished size of the gathered circle

Pattern C: The finished size of the square, padding and fabric square

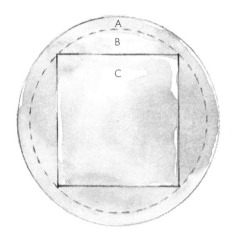

Use pattern guide A to cut out a fabric circle and pattern guide C to cut out one fabric square and one square of padding.

1. Choose contrasting fabrics for the squares and circles.

2. Gather the circle on the right side using running stitch along the outside edge of the fabric. Center pattern B on the wrong side of the fabric circle. Pull both thread ends to gather the fabric until the edges fold over the paper; tie the thread ends together with a double knot and press the edges of the fabric flat.

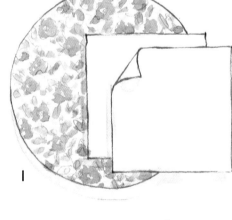

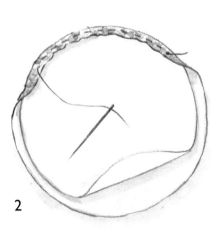

3. Remove this pattern and place pattern C on the wrong side of the circle, matching the fabric grain with the straight sides of the square.

4. Fold the edges of the circle over the square and press in the creases.

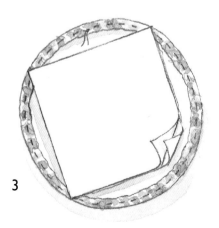

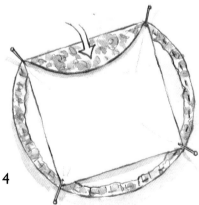

5. Remove the paper and insert the padding and fabric square. Refold the circle sides and pin the edges in place. Make sure the corners of the square are covered by the circle.

6. Quilt the edges using a running stitch through all the layers, starting and finishing on a curved side and not at the corners.

7. Lay out the finished squares in the order in which they are to be joined. Stitch together using slip stitch, aligning the outside folded edges, and stitching with the wrong sides together.

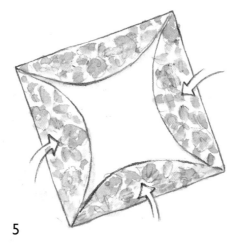

5

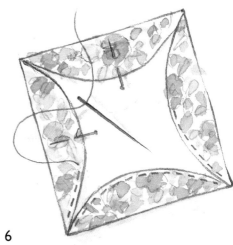

6

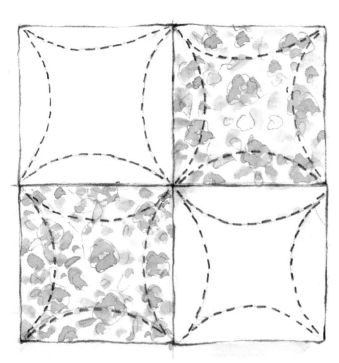

7

VARIATIONS TO THE CIRCLES

◆■◆■◆■◆■◆■◆■◆■◆■◆■◆■◆

The circles, like the large squares (pp.8–9), can be pieced to make halved or quartered pieces, which when joined, create additional patterns depending upon the order in which they are stitched (see the *Circus Cot Quilt* pp.72–76 and *Antique Flowers* quilt, pp.64–67).

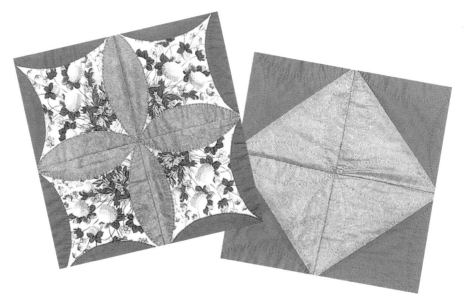

Hexagons

◆■◆■◆■◆■◆■◆■◆■◆■◆■◆■◆■◆■◆■◆■◆■

Following the same basic techniques for the squares (pp8–9), simple hexagon shapes can be used to make attractive patterns. Once the technique is mastered variations can be made to give flowers or stars.

PATTERN GUIDES
◆■◆■◆■◆■◆■◆■◆■◆■◆■◆■◆

Cut out paper pattern guides with these hexagons:

Pattern A: The size of the large hexagons when cut out

Pattern B: The finished size of the large hexagons and the cut size for padding

Pattern C: The size of the small hexagons when cut out

Pattern D: The finished size of the small hexagons

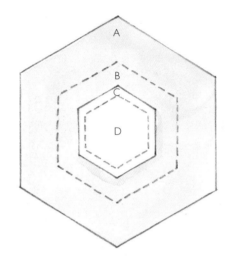

Cut two pieces of fabric using patterns A, and C, and one piece of padding using pattern B.

1. Place pattern B centrally on the wrong side of a large fabric hexagon. Fold the sides over the pattern and press in place.

2. Remove the pattern, place padding in the hexagon aligning the edges along the crease lines.

3. Refold the sides into the center and pin in place. Baste the corners with a backstitch to hold them in place when quilting.

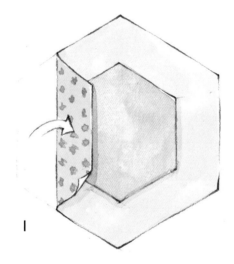

1

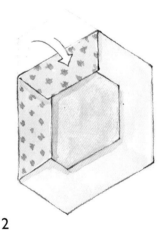

2

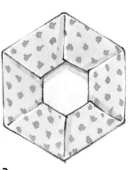

3

4. Center pattern D on the wrong side of a small fabric hexagon. Fold the edges of the fabric over the pattern and press in place.

5. Remove the pattern and place the small hexagon right side up onto the center of the large hexagon. Match the points with the mitered corners of the large hexagon and pin them together. Quilt the pieces together along the inside of the small hexagon. Start to stitch on a side, not on a point, with the thread end anchored between the layers. Finish in the same way.

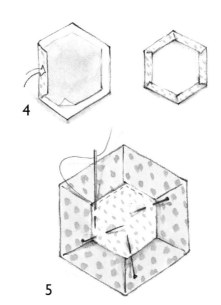

4

5

VARIATIONS TO HEXAGONS

The large hexagons can be made of halves or thirds to create additional patterns depending upon the order in which they are placed.

Basic Stitches

QUILTING STITCHES

Ladder stitch is used for sewing small squares, circles, or hexagons onto large ones when making basic patches. Stitch through the fold of the small piece and then through all the layers of the large piece. This stitch is invisible on one side and looks like quilting on the other side.

ladder stitch

Ladder stitch is also used to join patches together, in this instance they are squares. Gather the corners of four folded squares by taking a needle and thread through all four corners. Draw the thread through for half its length, leaving a long thread end, and tie a knot, pulling the threads very tightly at both ends. Fold the squares together in pairs with wrong sides facing, and pin the two ends of the squares. Ladder stitch pairs together with one of the long thread ends (half of the thread). Join two squares, use the other half of the thread. Open the squares out and refold to stitch the other sides of the pieces to make a block of four squares.

Quilting can be done by machine stitching, starting along the side and ending with three or four stitches overlapping. Leave about 6in of thread ends to pull through to one side. Thread a needle and run the ends between the layers to finish.

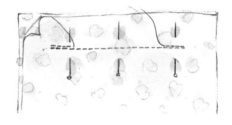

machine stitch

VARIATIONS IN JOINING

Running stitch can be used to join large pieces before the padding is inserted. After the finished size is marked with creases, unfold the pieces, match the right sides and pin the creases together. Stitch on the wrong side along the creases with running stitch. Make an extra backstitch at the corners to reinforce the points.

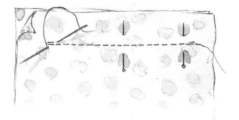

running stitch

Machine stitched joining is done in the same way as the running stitch method. The large pieces are stitched before the padding and smaller pieces are put together. When stitched by machine, the corners of the squares may need to be gathered to tighten the joins.

MITERING

This technique is used for neatening fabric ends at corners. Fold the corner diagonally so that the fold line meets that of the hem. Cut the corner. Fold the hems in and pin in place to secure them while you ladder stitch them together.

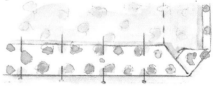

Projects

Bandanas and Jeans

This is an easy and fun quilt to make which is suitable for a boy's bed or as a picnic blanket. The bandanas are already hemmed ready to be folded, and will not all, therefore, be exactly the same size. They are folded to make 14 in. squares with a large turning allowance. The jean patches are inserted under the edges of the bandanas.

Finished quilt size: 70 inches square

YOU WILL NEED

Materials
- ◆ 25 red and white bandanas, 21 in. square
- ◆ 25 scraps of old jeans (including seams and pockets), 8 in. square
- ◆ cotton flannel sheet, single bed size

Pattern Guides
- ● A   14 in. square
- ● B   8 in. square

Paste the 14 in. pattern guide onto lightweight card and cut a 12 in. square hole in it to make a window. Cut the card using a matte knife and metal ruler.

Number of pieces to cut
- ■ A   25 × cotton flannel squares
- ■ B   25 × scraps of old jeans

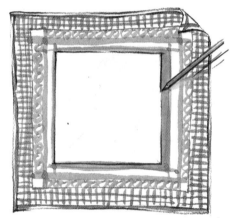

1. Place the window template on the wrong side of the bandanas, centering the square on the printed pattern. Mark stitch lines with a marking pencil or tailors' chalk around the outside of the template.

2. Lay out the bandanas to decide the order in which they are to be joined. It is a good idea to number them at this stage so they can be picked up and stitched easily and without confusion.

Bandanas and Jeans color chart

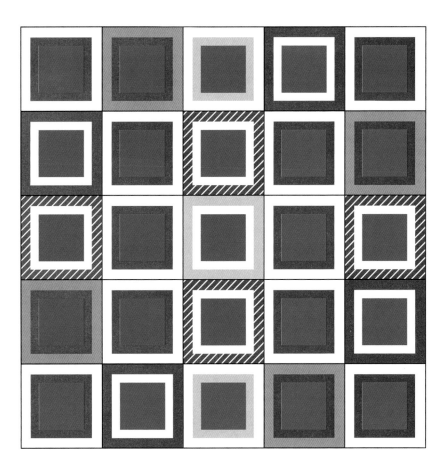

front

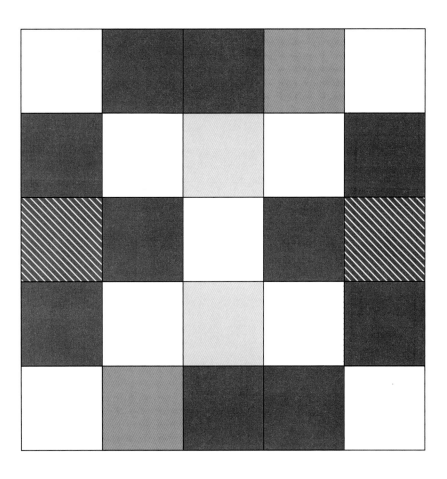

back

3. If any of the pieces are of a lighter weight fabric than the others, it will be easier to stitch and fold them if they are spray starched.

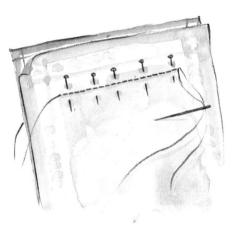

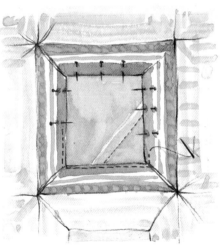

5. When all the bandanas are stitched, lay out the whole quilt with the flaps right side up, ready to be folded. Insert the padding in the squares and fold the corners into the center.

4. The bandanas are sewn together before the folded squares are made. Align the marked lines of adjacent bandanas and machine stitch, leaving long threads at both ends of the stitching. Pull the ends through to one side, thread a needle with both ends and make two backstitches to reinforce the corners.

7. Fold the four sides of the bandana over the edges of the jeans and pin in place. Baste the squares and quilt by machine or hand with running stitch.

6. Center the jean patches over the padding. Lift the points of the bandanas out and over the jeans.

Batik

◆■◆◆■◆◆■◆◆■◆◆■◆◆■◆◆■◆◆■◆◆■◆◆■◆◆■◆◆■◆◆■◆◆■◆◆■◆◆■◆◆■

OVERLAPPING SQUARES ARE CREATED BY GATHERING THE CORNERS OF THE SQUARES AND TYING A TIGHT KNOT TO HOLD THEM TOGETHER. THE DESIGN USES A SQUARE INSIDE A SQUARE WITH ADDITIONAL IMPACT GIVEN BY ALTERNATING COLORS AND PATTERNS. SOME OF THE BATIKED PATTERN WAS CHOSEN TO MAKE A TURNING EFFECT. OTHER SQUARES PICKED OUT FISH AND TURTLE DESIGNS IN THE FABRICS TO LOOK AS IF THEY ARE SWIMMING AROUND.

FINISHED QUILT SIZE: 80 INCHES SQUARE

YOU WILL NEED

Materials
◆ plain white cotton 6 yd × 48 in.
◆ navy blue 3 yd 28 in. × 48 in.
◆ medium blue 3 yd 22 in. × 48 in.
◆ batik—five patterns of at least 1 yd × 48 in.
◆ cotton flannel 4 yd 29 in. × 48 in. or use a double bed size sheet
◆ iron-on interlining 2 yd 14 in. × 36½ in.

Pattern Guides
● A   21 in. square
● B   16 in. square
● C   13 in. square
● D   12 in. square
● E   5 in. square
● F   4 in. square
● G   5 in. square, with a window, or hole, of 4 in. square

Number of pieces to cut
■ A   12 × plain white cotton
       13 × navy blue
■ B   25 × cotton flannel
■ C   13 × plain white cotton
       12 × medium blue
■ E   48 × plain white cotton
       52 × medium blue
       100 × batik
■ F   200 × iron-on interlining

1. Mark the stitch lines, 2½ in. in from the edge, on the wrong side of the navy squares. Fold and press along these lines. Mark stitch lines 2½ in. on the right side of the large white squares using pattern B.

2. Match the fold of a navy square to the stitch line of the white square. Open the fold and pin the pieces together. Machine stitch from point to point leaving long thread ends. Pull the ends through to the navy side, thread both onto the needle and make two backstitches to reinforce the corners.

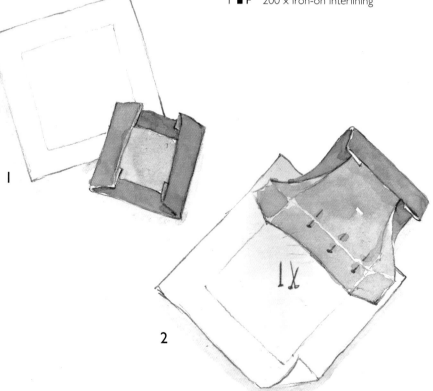

2

3. Make five rows of alternating colors and stitch the rows together with ladder stitch.

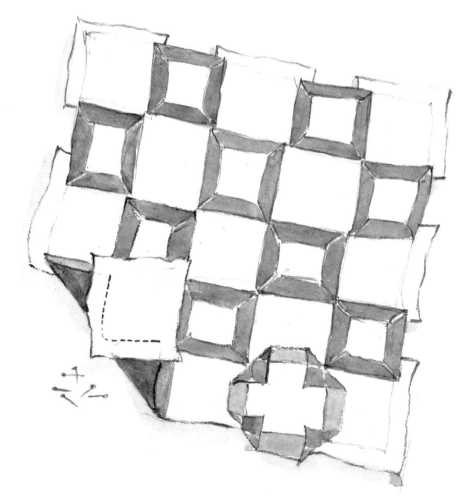

4. Lay the quilt out and fold the alternate squares facing you, following the Basic Techniques pp.8–9. Insert a 16 in. square of padding and press the folds of the corners and flaps, then pin and baste.

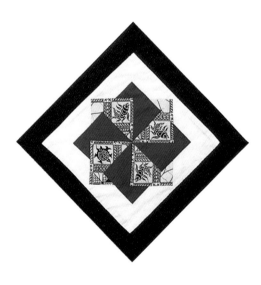

Batik color charts

The color variations shown in these charts indicate how the different batik patterns are used.

front

back

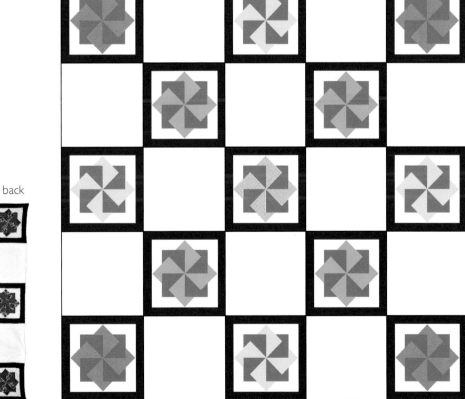

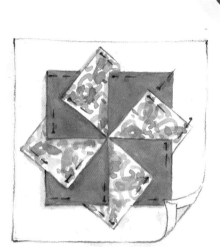

5. To ensure that a particular part of the batik pattern appears in the corners of the overlapping squares, use the window of pattern G. The design desired for the corners may mean that the fabric is cut on the bias, so apply iron-on interlining to the wrong side of the squares to make the batik fabric square and give the white fabric body. Press the turnings to the back and baste.

7. Spread the squares out again, slip the top one under the last one so that they all overlap. Pin the corners of the squares to the ones underneath. Center a batik square on each of the background squares, alternating between white and medium blue.

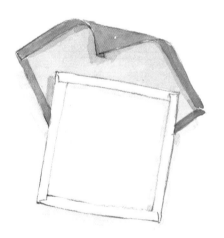

6. Lay out the batik squares in the order in which they are to be joined. Gather the corners together and tie with a tight knot on the wrong side.

8. Sew around the edges of the pieces with ladder stitch to join them to the background. Press the turnings of the background square to the back using the pattern D.

9. Place these squares onto the larger squares matching the points to the mitered corners. Position the white inner squares on the navy frames and the medium blue squares on the white frames. Quilt by hand using white quilting thread on the white squares and navy quilting thread on the blue squares. Also quilt around the batik squares with navy quilting thread on the medium blue, along the appliqued edges of the turning squares.

Wallhanging

This Japanese-style double-sided wallhanging is made of five equal squares that are joined with braid and wooden beads. Because it is double-sided it can be hung in an open space like a wide doorway, in a glass panel, or in a stairwell. Alternatively, it may be hung on a wall and turned depending on the seasonal light or the desire for a change.

Finished size hanging length: 60 × 9 inches

YOU WILL NEED

Materials

- ◆ ivory cotton, 40 × 48 in.
- ◆ apricot check, 18 × 36 in.
- ◆ selection of fabrics for strips—scraps or 18 × 18 in. squares
- ◆ cotton flannel, 18 × 36 in.
- ◆ four brown wooden and four blue ceramic beads
- ◆ braid, 2 yd
- ◆ bamboo skewers, 10 in. long. Cut off points for the 9 in. required

Pattern Guides

- ● A   13 in. square
- ● B   9 in. square
- ● C   8 × 8½ in. piece
- ● D   7 in. square

The following patterns are used to make the strips:

- ● E   8 in. × various sizes
- ● F   7 × 13 in.

Number of square pieces to cut

- ■ A   five × ivory cotton
- ■ B   five × cotton flannel for padding
- ■ C   five × apricot check

1. Cut fabric strips 8 in. wide in various lengths, adding a ½ in. seam allowance around the edges. Cut enough strips to make two lengths when the strips are sewn together—one of 65 in. and one of 40 in. Machine stitch the strips together across the 8 in. widths, press the seams closed, all facing in one direction.

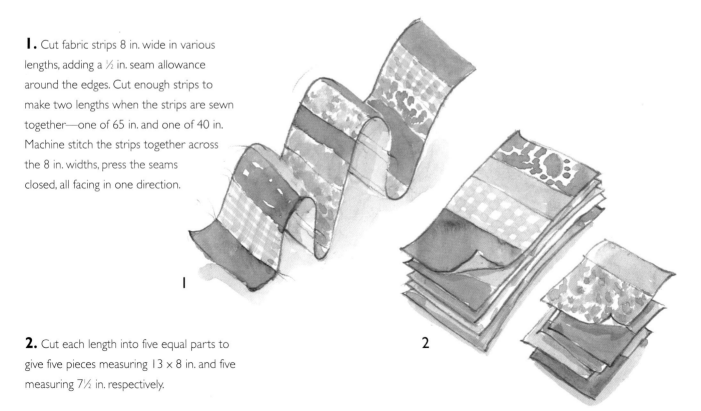

2. Cut each length into five equal parts to give five pieces measuring 13 × 8 in. and five measuring 7½ in. respectively.

3. Fold back the long sides of each of the larger strips by ½ in. and pin each piece to the right side of an ivory square. Center the small stripped pieces on the right side of the apricot squares, folding the raw edges under. Pin in place.

4. Ladder stitch the folded edges of all of the squares. (Using the full-size pieces of fabric behind the strips gives the lightweight and open-weave fabrics additional support when hanging. This is also why the strips are handsewn—they could be machine stitched to the larger pieces if all the fabrics are the same weight.)

5. Press the squares flat, turn all the edges of the large square back ½ in. and press in place. Fold the square using pattern B and following the Basic Techniques pp.8–9.

3

4

5

6. Keep following the basic techniques to assemble the large and small squares, inserting a 9 in. bamboo skewer along the fold lines at the top and bottom of each square before placing the small square on top. Fold the edges of the large square over those of the small square before ladder-stitching.

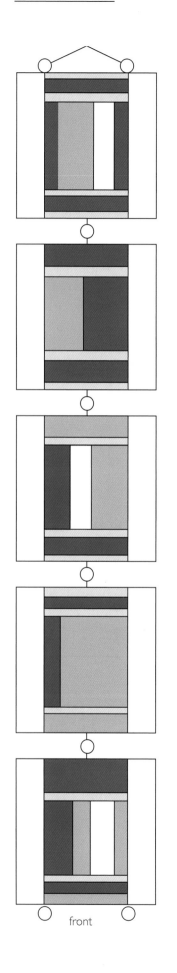

front

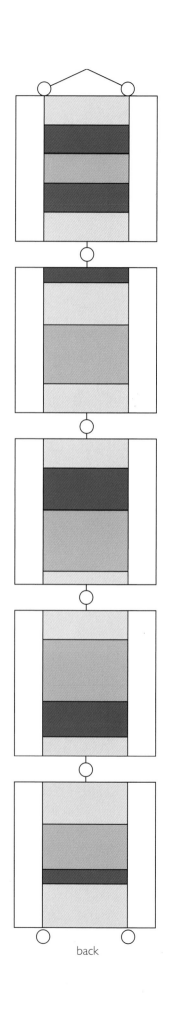

back

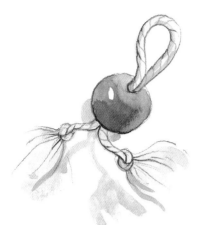

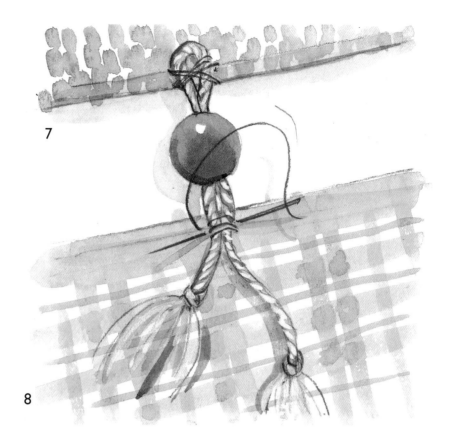

7

8

7. To join the squares use lengths of braid threaded through the wooden beads. Cut four 10 in. lengths, fold in half and pull a loop through each of the beads. Knot both ends of the braid about 2 in. from the cut ends. Move the bead so the top of the loop is about 1½ in. long.

8. Place a pin to mark the middle of the top and bottom of the squares to be joined. Stitch the braid onto the back using a cross stitch worked over the braid and under the skewer that is between the layers. Make four or five cross stitches in each direction. Anchor the end of the thread with some small backstitches behind the crossed ones. Repeat the process to hold the other end of the braid to the top of the next block. Untwist the loose ends of the braid up to the knots, and trim to the desired length.

9. To hang the wallhanging, use a length of braid with two ceramic beads at each end. Cut an 18 in. length of braid, thread the beads onto each end and knot both in place about 3 in. from the ends. Stitch the braid to the 7 in. join in the stripped piece. Stitch in place with cross stitch as before. Unravel the ends of the braid and trim. Add a 14 in. length of braid across the bottom of the wallhanging, couching it just above the folded edge or along a join in the strip pieces. Add two ceramic beads to the ends, hold in place with knots and unravel the ends as before. The beads help to balance the wallhanging especially if it is hung in a free standing place.

9

Crosses and Diamonds

This quilt is made of one hundred 5 inch squares, with some of the large squares made by joining two triangles. When folded and sewn together they create a cross effect on one side and a diamond one on the other side. The border is made by using the patterned fabric for the small squares.

Finished quilt size: 50 inches square

YOU WILL NEED

Materials

- ◆ plain white cotton, 7 yd × 36 in.
- ◆ printed cotton, 2½ yd × 36 in.
- ◆ cotton flannel padding, 2½ yd × 36 in.

Pattern Guides

- ● A 7½ in. square
- ● B 5 in. square
- ● C 4 in. square
- ● D 3 in. square
- ● E 8 × 8 × 11¼ in. triangle

Number of pieces to cut

- ■ A 64 × plain white cotton
- ■ B 100 × cotton flannel padding
- ■ C 72 × plain white cotton and
       28 × printed cotton
- ■ E 36 × printed cotton and
       36 × plain white cotton

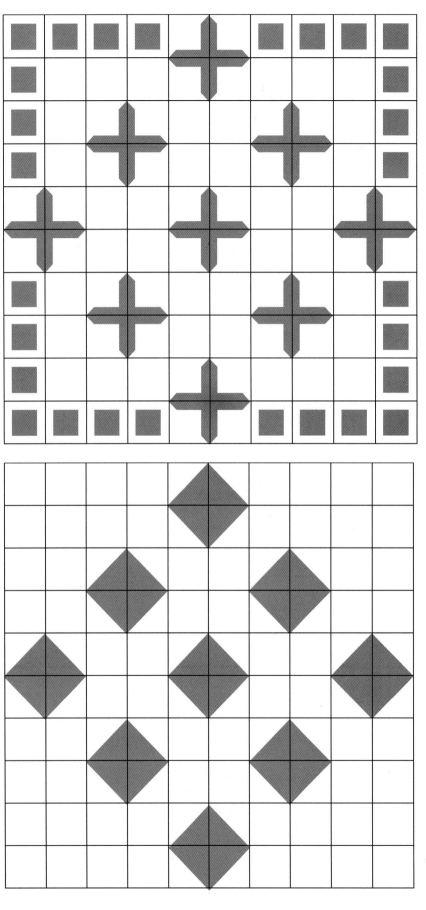

1. Make up the squares (see Basic Techniques, pp.10–11), with the printed small squares placed on white large squares and the white small squares on the pieced and plain large squares. Stitch together using white quilting thread with quilting stitch worked along the folded edges. To make the squares from triangles, mark the seam line on the wrong side of the printed cotton triangle. Pin one plain and one printed piece together along the marked line. Stitch by hand using an even running stitch. Press the seam closed and to one side of the triangles in order to get a sharp point when the square is folded.

2. Build the quilt up by joining four squares together with a gathering stitch and knot (see Basic Techniques, pp.14–15).

3. A checkerboard effect is produced on the back by the diamond block of four squares.

4. Follow the layout pattern for the order in which the squares are joined.

Crosses and Diamonds color charts
front (above) back (below)

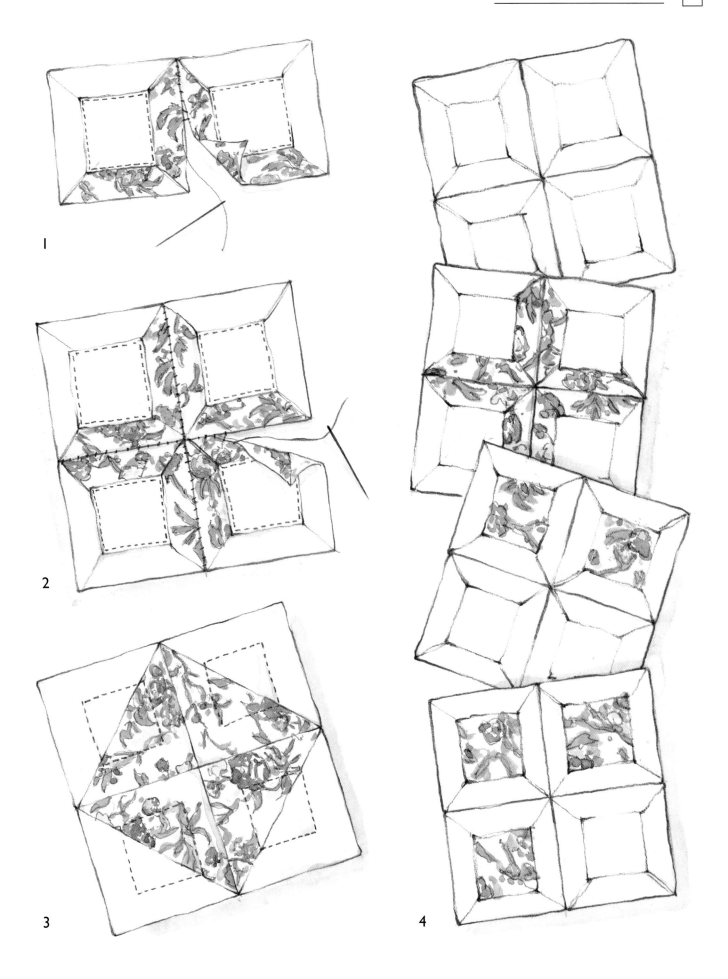

1

2

3

4

Roman Stripes

◆■◆■◆◆■◆◆■◆◆■◆◆■◆◆■◆◆■◆◆■◆◆■◆◆■◆◆■◆◆■◆◆■◆■◆

ROMAN STRIPES ARE A TRADITIONAL AMERICAN PATCHWORK PATTERN, MADE WITH
STRIPS TO MAKE A DIAGONAL STRIPE ACROSS ONE CORNER OF A SQUARE. FOR THIS
QUILT THE PATTERN HAS BEEN ADAPTED USING PRINTED STRIPES AND ENLARGED TO
BRING THE SIDES AROUND TO THE OTHER SIDE TO FORM A FOLDED BLOCK. IN THE
CENTER OF THE SMALLER SQUARE THERE ARE TWO ADDITIONAL SQUARES TO MAKE A
DIAMOND AND SQUARE EFFECT.

FINISHED QUILT SIZE: 48 INCHES SQUARE

YOU WILL NEED

Materials

◆ printed stripes and blue cotton,
  78 x 48 in. each
◆ plain white cotton, 20 x 36 in.
◆ cotton flannel, 48 in. square

Pattern Guides

● A 12 in. square
● B 11 in. square
● C 10 in. square
● D   8 in. square
● E   7 in. square
● F   6 in. square
● G   5 in. square
● H 15 x 15 x 21½ in. triangle

Number of pieces to cut

■ A 16 x cotton flannel padding
■ B 16 x plain white cotton
■ D 16 x blue
■ F 16 x striped cotton
■ H 16 x striped cotton and
     16 x blue triangles

1. Cut the triangles with the stripes running
parallel to the hypotenuse of the pattern.
Lay out the blue triangles with the selvage
parallel to the hypotenuse to match the
striped fabric. Pin the right sides together
along the seam line and machine stitch. Press
the seam closed to one side of the square.

2. Use pattern B to fold the pieced square
following instructions in Basic Techniques,
pp.8–9. Insert the padding at this stage.

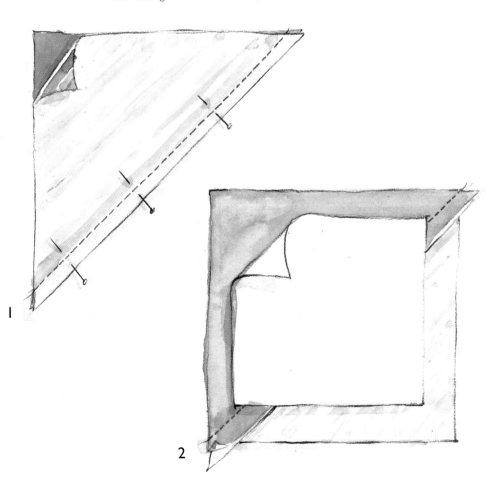

3. Lay the pieced square down with the folded sides facing upward. Fold all three inner squares to their finished sizes. Place them on the folded square, starting with the white one squared, just as you would following the Basic Techniques, pp.8–9. Quilt along the folded edges.

4. Place the small blue square, on the point, centering it on the white square, and quilt in place.

5. Finally center the striped square on the blue square—this time squared. Following the chart for the direction of the stripes, quilt along the folded edges.

6. Ladder stitch the squares together: join the two striped sides to form a chevron. Repeat this join for the eight pairs, then continue following the layout pattern.

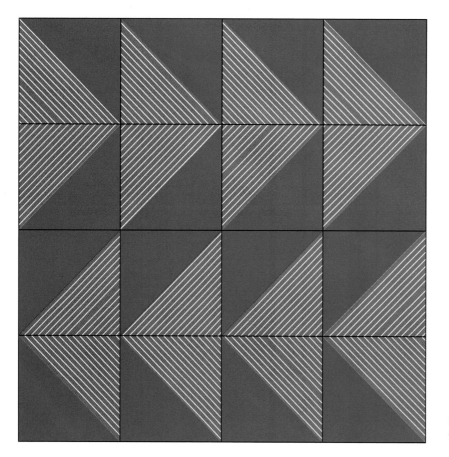

Roman Stripes color charts
front (above), back (below)

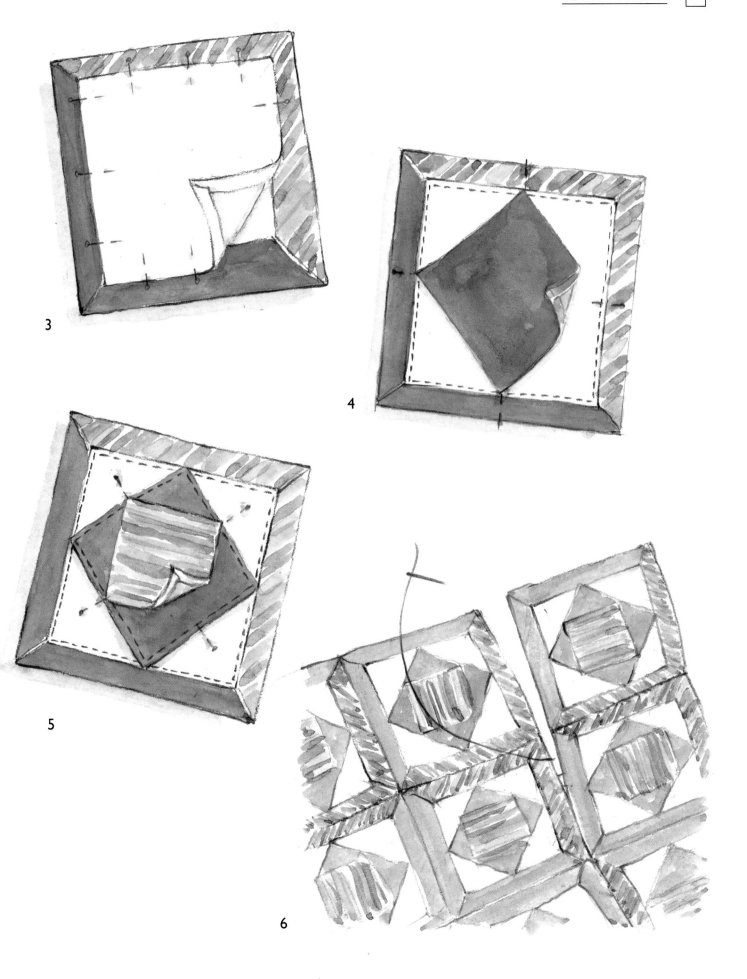

3

4

5

6

Handkerchiefs

◆■□◆■□◆■□◆■□◆■□◆■□◆■□◆■□◆■□◆■□◆■□◆■□◆■□◆■□◆■□◆■◆

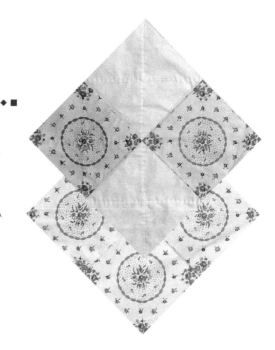

This design is built up from a center of 16 old-fashioned-style handkerchiefs, each folded into a square and assembled to make a cot-size quilt. By adding the corner pieces and larger squares to make a border, the quilt can grow with the child. To enlarge it further, add two more rows of the larger squares to the top and bottom to make a full size single bed quilt.

Finished quilt size: 56 inches square

YOU WILL NEED

Materials
- ◆ 24 old-fashioned handkerchiefs with colored borders, 10 in. square
- ◆ eight patterned handkerchiefs, 10 in. square
- ◆ plain white cotton, 3 yd × 48 in.
- ◆ cotton flannel padding 3 yd × 36 in.

Pattern Guides
- ● A   17 in. square
- ● B   14 in. square
- ● C   10½ in. square
- ● D   7 in. square

Number of pieces to cut
- ■ A   eight × white cotton
- ■ B   eight × flannel padding
- ■ C   eight × white cotton
- ■ D   32 × flannel padding

1. Press the handkerchiefs flat, place a 7 in. padding square turned on the point across the center of each handkerchief with a colored border. Fold each point of the handkerchief into the center like an envelope and pin the join through all the layers.

2. Quilt across each square starting from the center and stitching out to the corners. Cut a long piece of thread and pull half the length through the center. Using one long thread end, stitch outward to finish at the corner. Thread the other thread end and stitch to the opposite corner. Repeat this process for the other two sides.

3. To make the eight small white squares, turn the outside edges under ¼ in. and press in place. Machine stitch around the edges. Fold these squares in the same manner as the handkerchiefs, and quilt.

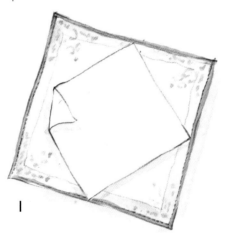

1

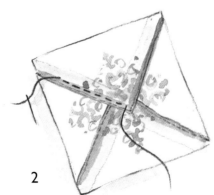

2

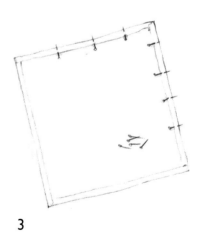

3

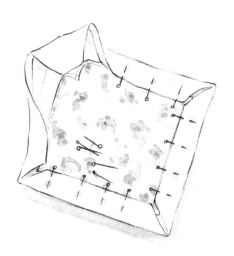

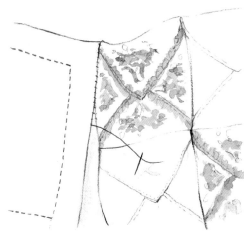

5. Place the finished squares in the order in which they are to be joined and ladder stitch them together.

4. To make the larger squares, fold the 17 in. squares into a finished size of 14 in. square in the same way as before. Insert the other handkerchiefs in position under the edge of the larger square. Turn the raw edges of the large squares under, pin in place and quilt. Because this is a child's quilt it is a good idea to ladder stitch the corners closed.

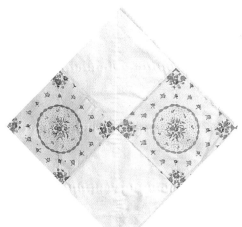

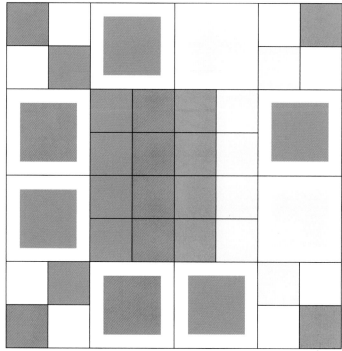

Handkerchiefs color charts

front

back

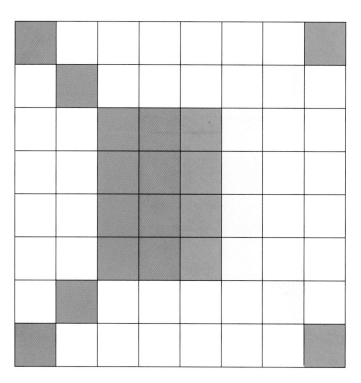

Windows

THIS IS A PATCHWORK PIECED BLOCK WITH A THREE-DIMENSIONAL QUALITY. ONE SIDE HAS A BROWN SQUARE IN·THE CENTER TO MAKE THE ILLUSION STRONGER THAN ON THE OTHER SIDE. THE QUILT CAN BE MADE IN ANY COLOR AS LONG AS THE SHADES OF THE COLORS ARE THE SAME AS ILLUSTRATED. USE A LIGHT AND MEDIUM SHADE OF THE SAME COLOR FOR THE PATCHWORK PIECES AND A DARK ONE FOR THE INSIDE SQUARE.

FINISHED QUILT SIZE: 48 × 60 INCHES

YOU WILL NEED

Materials
◆ chintz and checks, 2¼ yd × 45 in. each (pink chintz and pink checks; rust chintz and beige checks)
◆ brown printed cotton, 40 × 45 in.
◆ cotton flannel padding, 60 × 48 in. or a single bed sheet

Pattern Guides
● A   12 in. square
● B   7 in. square
● C   6 in. square

Trace pattern guides for the pieced large square using the templates D, E, F, and G on pp.100–102

Number of pieces to cut
■ A   20 × padding
■ B   20 × dark brown
■ D   20 × pink chintz
■ E   20 × beige check
■ F   20 × rust chintz
■ G   20 × pink check

1. Piece the large square, joining the triangles to the trapezoid shapes first. Joining D to E and F to G.

2. Then join these two large triangles to make the square. Press the seams closed and to one side of the pieces.

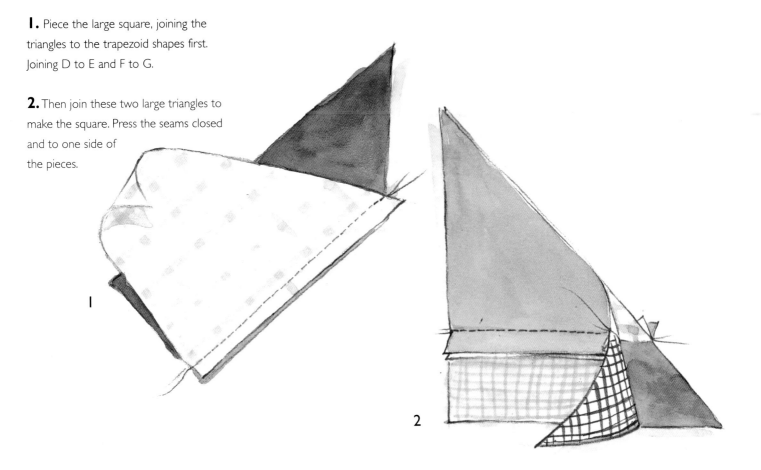

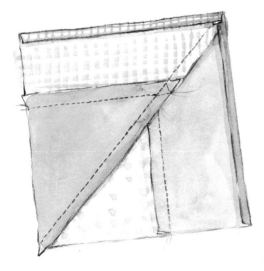

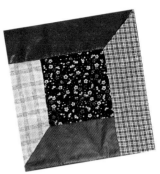

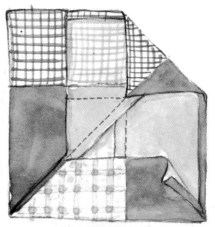

3. With the pieced square face down, turn under the two pink edges ½ in. and press in place. Fold the top edge under, matching the fold to the seam on the wrong side and press in place.

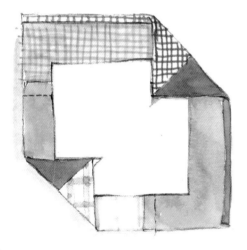

4. Open out and place pattern A on the crease, matching the top left hand corner with the diagonal seam line.

5. Fold the bottom right and top left hand corners of the square as in Basic Techniques, pp.8–9 to give mitered corners.

7. For the small square, place pattern C in the center of the wrong side of the fabric square and fold back the edges on the bottom and the right sides only. Press, remove the pattern and place on the large square right side up. The folded edges will cover the turning on the left side and the bottom of the large square.

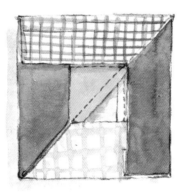

6. The other corners are folded with straight sides out to the folded sides. Press all the folds in place, remove the pattern and insert padding. Refold the edges and pin or baste in place.

8. Pin in place. Slip the other two sides under the other two sides of the large square and pin in place.

Windows color charts

front   back

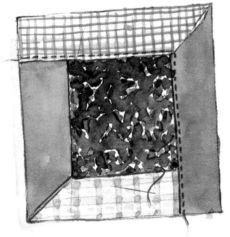

9. Machine quilt along the inside of the folded edges of the small square and the outside of the large square, leaving long enough thread ends to finish between the layers.

10. Ladder stitch the straight ends closed before joining the squares. Use ladder stitch to join the squares in pairs and blocks in the order described in Basic Techniques, pp.14–15.

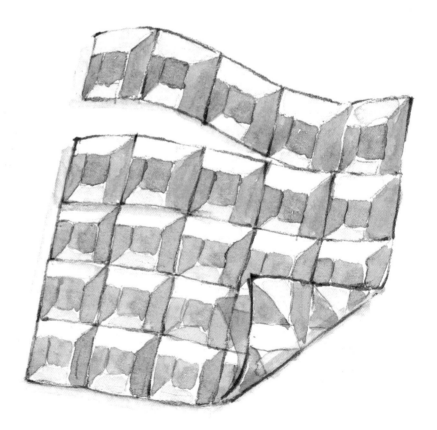

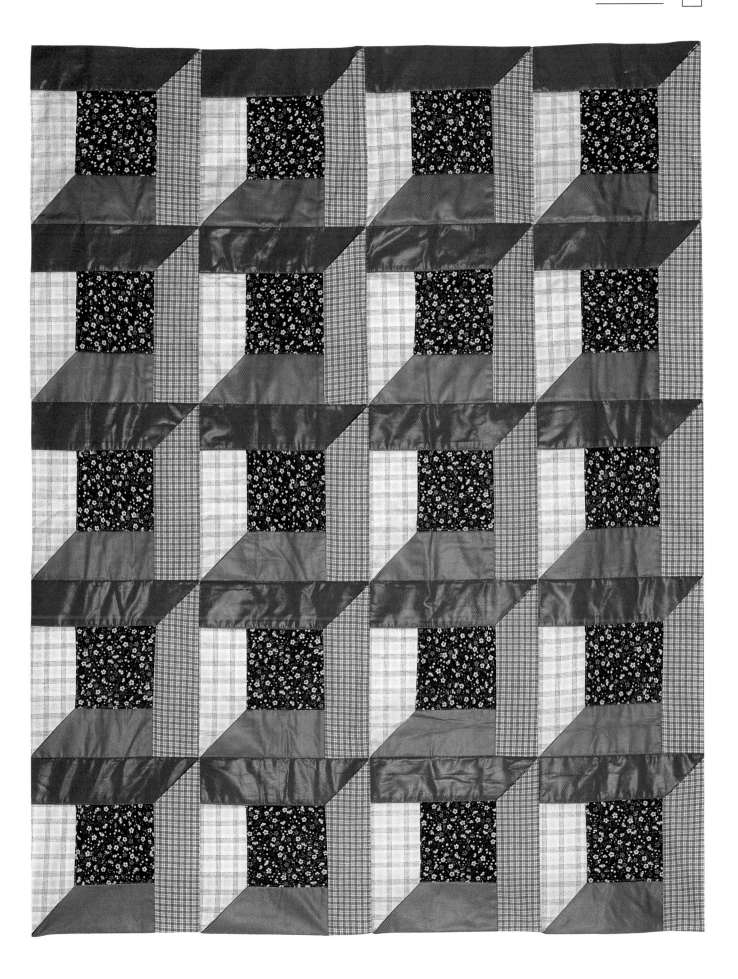

Victorian Tiles

VICTORIAN TILES HAVE INSPIRED THE CHOICE OF COLORS FOR THIS QUILT. THE PATCHWORK PATTERN IS A TRADITIONAL AMERICAN NINE PATCH DESIGN CALLED VARIABLE STAR, LONE STAR, MOSAIC PATCHWORK AND FLYING CROW.

FINISHED QUILT SIZE: 64 INCHES SQUARE

YOU WILL NEED

Materials

- ◆ chintz: rust and light gold, 60 × 42 in. each
- ◆ peach and dark gold, 80 × 42 in. each
- ◆ printed gold, 15 × 40 in.
- ◆ printed red, 24 × 42 in.
- ◆ plaids: two dark colors, 12 × 42 in. each
- ◆ plaids: two light colors, 24 × 42 in. each
- ◆ cotton flannel sheet, single bed size

Pattern Guides

- ● A 12¾ in. square
- ● B 10½ in. square
- ● C   9½ in. square

Trace pattern guides for the pieced large square using the templates on p.103. Cut the fabrics out, making a 17¾ in. square to be folded.

Number of pieces to cut

- ■ A 25 × cotton flannel padding
- ■ B five × printed red
     four each of dark plaids
     six each of light plaids
- ■ D 25 × printed gold
- ■ E 100 × peach
- ■ F 100 × light gold
     200 × dark gold
- ■ G 100 × rust

1. Join the pieces of the large square in the order of the diagram using machine stitch. Press the seams closed as they are stitched. Mark the seam lines on the wrong side of the pieced squares with a marking pencil.

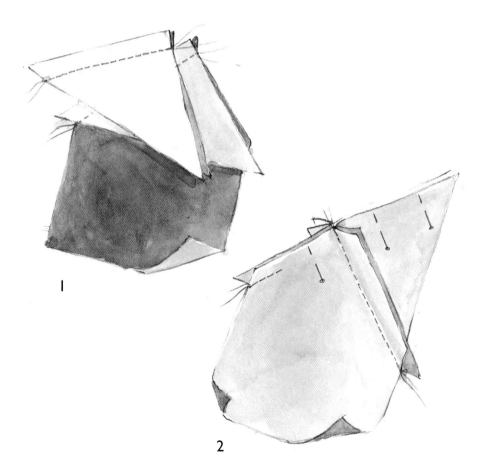

1

2

2. Assemble each large square using the layout pattern on page 48 as a guide.

3. When you have finished stitching, place the pieced block flat with flaps wrong side up. Insert the paddings into the squares. Fold the corners and then the sides into the centers, ready for the inner squares to be placed.

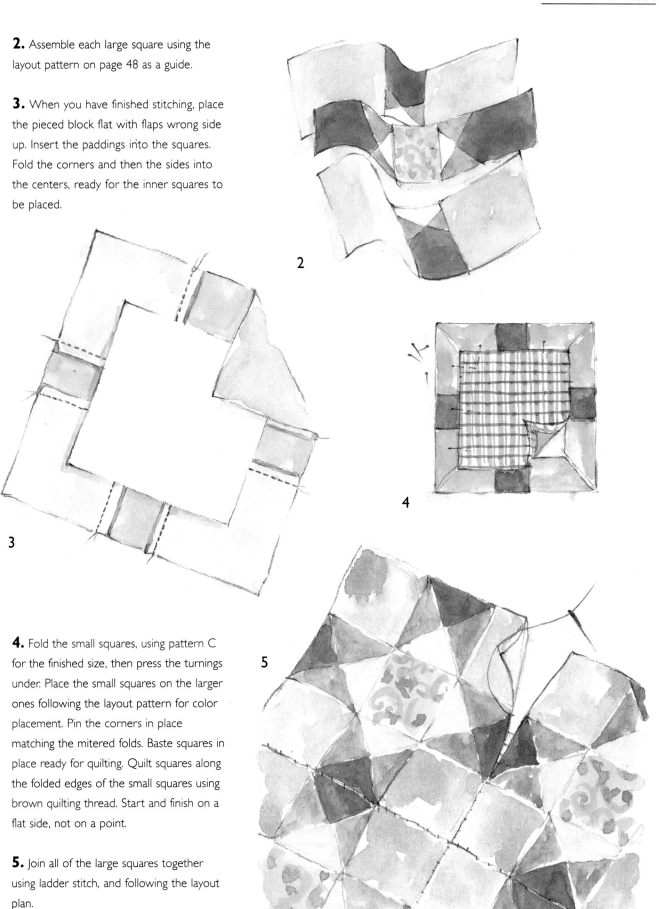

2

3

4

5

4. Fold the small squares, using pattern C for the finished size, then press the turnings under. Place the small squares on the larger ones following the layout pattern for color placement. Pin the corners in place matching the mitered folds. Baste squares in place ready for quilting. Quilt squares along the folded edges of the small squares using brown quilting thread. Start and finish on a flat side, not on a point.

5. Join all of the large squares together using ladder stitch, and following the layout plan.

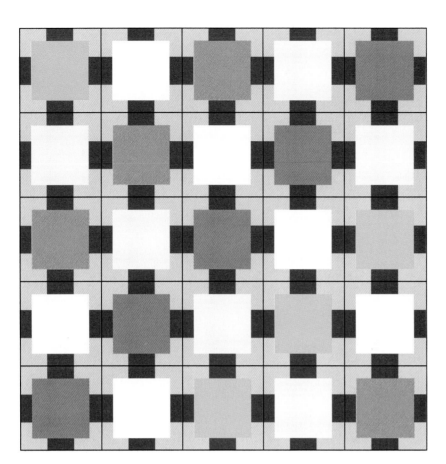

Victorian Tiles color charts
front

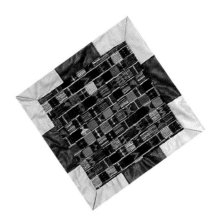

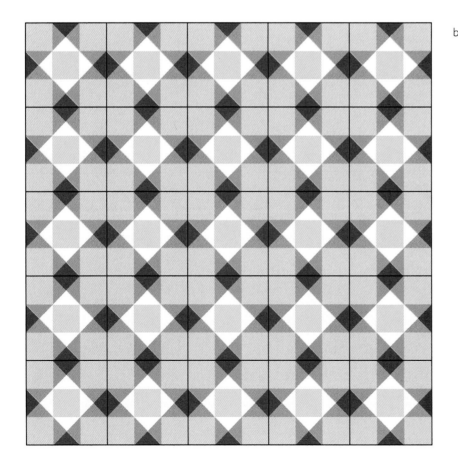

back

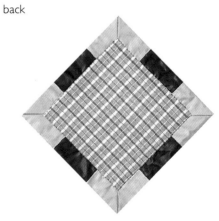

Numbers and Alphabets

This is a bright, cheerful quilt that can be used on either side to help children learn colors, numbers, and letters as well as keeping them warm. The numbers and letters are appliquéd in place with zigzag machine stitching. The large squares are all pieced triangles and four of the small squares are also pieced.

Finished quilt size: 64 inches square

YOU WILL NEED

Materials

◆ yellow, red, green, and blue cotton, 2 yd × 45 in. each
◆ white printed fabric for letters, 18 × 42 in.
◆ miscellaneous patterned fabrics for numbers, scraps of at least 5 in. squares
◆ cotton flannel padding, single bed sheet
◆ iron-on interfacing 18 × 36 in.
◆ sewing thread—yellow, red, green, and blue
◆ quilting thread—white

Pattern Guides

● A 21 in. square
● B 16 in. square
● C 13 in. square
● D 12 in. square
● E 21½ × 21½ × 31½ in. triangle
● F 10 × 10 × 14 in. triangle

Number of pieces to cut

■ B 16 × cotton flannel padding
■ C 12 × plain white cotton
■ E eight × yellow, red, green and blue
■ F four × yellow, red, green and blue

Trace or photocopy the letters and numbers from the templates provided on pp.104–109. Trace the outline of the letters and numbers onto the shiny side of the iron-on interfacing. Cut out the shapes from the interfacing and fix them onto the wrong side of the fabrics, using printed white for the letters and mixed colors for the numbers. Follow the edge of the interfacing on the wrong side of the fabric with a narrow and not very solid zigzag stitch. Stitch around the inside shapes with the same stitch size. Use white thread for the letters and a matching color for the numbers—for example, green on green. Pull the thread ends to the wrong side and trim. Cut out the letters and numbers using stitches as a guide.

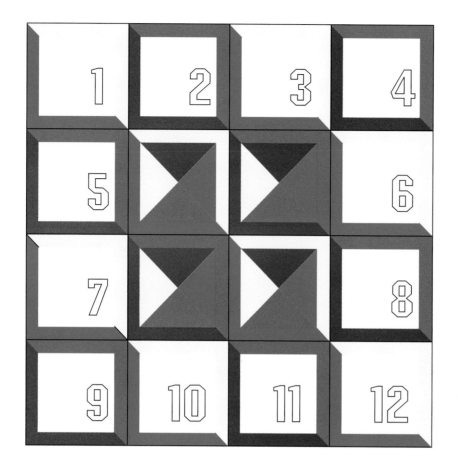

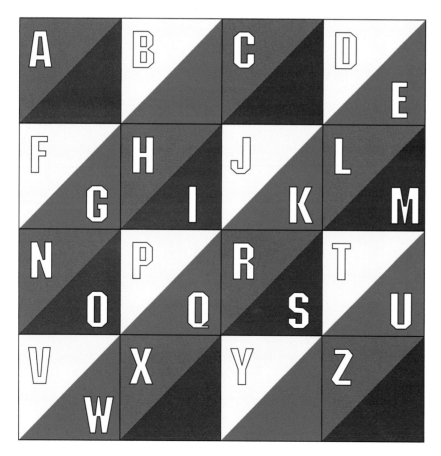

1. Cut out triangles of fabric using patterns E and F. Following the chart, stitch the triangles together to make the large and small squares. Press the seams closed and to one side of the squares.

2. Mark the squares for the placement of the letters and numbers by cutting windows in patterns B and D. The top left-hand corner of your letter or number box should be 3 in. from the top left-hand corner of the large square—measured on the diagonal axis. Lay the fabric pieces right side up, place the full pattern over the fabric and put the letters in the window, matching the top, bottom and the right side to the 4 in. line.

Numbers and Alphabets color charts front (above), back (below)

3. Pin in place, stitch with white thread and a slightly wider zigzag stitch over the previous stitches, including the inside shapes of the letters. Then pull the ends of the threads to the back and trim.

5. Fold the numbered and pieced small squares to the finished size using pattern D, then press the folds. Remove the paper pattern and place the small squares over the corners of the large squares. Pin in place. Stitch both squares together with ladder stitch using white quilting thread. Ladder stitch into the fold of the smaller square and then through all the layers to the other side. The stitch will not be seen on the top and will look like a quilting stitch on the back.

6. Join in pairs as described in Basic Techniques, pp. 14–15. Then join pairs together to make four strips of four squares.

7. Sew each row of squares together using ladder stitch, ensuring the alphabet letters and numbers remain consecutive.

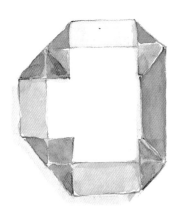

4. When the letters are stitched, use pattern B to fold the seams to the wrong side of the large square. Remove the pattern, and insert the padding.

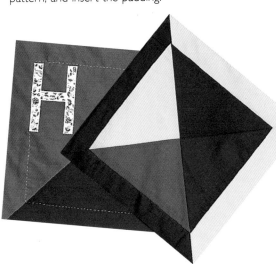

Butterflies

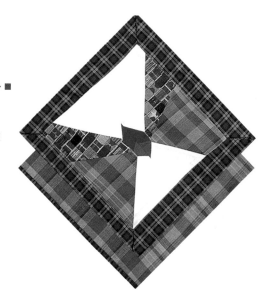

On this quilt the inner squares are pieced with irregular shapes that create an impression of the flight or movement of a butterfly. There are four different blocks that are made four times to give sixteen designs. You may want to try to make your own butterflies. These designs were made by folding a paper square vertically three times and horizontally four times, then unfolding it and drawing lines along the creases to make the pattern for the pieces.

Finished quilt size: 64 inches square

YOU WILL NEED

Materials

◆ blue and green printed plaid 3 yd × 48 in.

◆ four multi-colored plaids 40 × 45 in. each (squares A, B, C, and D)

◆ blue printed pattern 18 × 36 in. (pieces 3 and 15)

◆ plain white 18 × 36 in.

◆ blue, green, red, and yellow scraps or fat quarters 18 in. square

◆ cotton flannel sheet for padding, single bed size

◆ navy quilting thread

Pattern Guides

Make paper pattern guides of butterflies that are marked A, B, C, and D with the numbered pieces (see templates on pp.110–125)

● E 21 in. square

● F 16 in. square

● G 12 in. square

Number of pieces to cut

■ E eight × blue and green printed plaid two × each of other plaids

■ F 16 × cotton flannel padding

For butterflies cut four of each piece

■ 1, 4, 5, 8, 9, 12, 13, and 16 are plain white

■ 2 and 4 are plaids A, B, C, and D

■ 3 and 5 are blue printed cotton

■ 6 and 10 are plain blue

■ 7 and 11 are yellow with A, green with B, red with C, and green with D plaids

1. The butterfly patterns in the book are reduced in scale to 75%. For the full size, enlarge them on a photocopier. Trace around each pattern separately, adding a ¼ in. seam allowance to all the sides. While tracing, mark all pieces with the letter and number on the pattern as well as the arrow marking the straight grain of the fabric. Photocopy the paper tracings, cut out the copied patterns and keep the original tracing in one piece for reference while stitching.

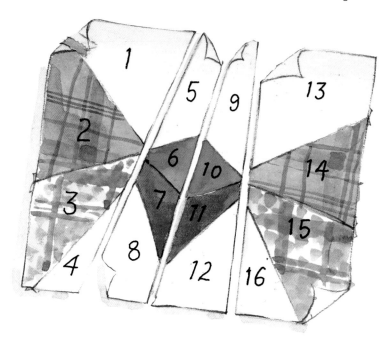

2. Pin the patterns on the right side of the fabrics for cutting. Cut four of each piece to make the 16 squares. Lay out the squares following the order marked on the guides on pp. 110–125. Stitch the pieces in numerical order from 1 to 4, 5 to 8, 9 to 12, and 13 to 16. Press the seams closed. On the first and third strip press them downward, and on the second and fourth strip press them upward. Stitch the strips together to complete the block. Repeat these directions for squares B, C, and D.

3. Place the squares face down, center the finished size pattern G on the squares and press the turnings to the back. Fold the large squares with the padding following the instructions in Basic Techniques, pp. 8–9.

4. Follow the color order on the layout pattern. Pin the butterfly and folded squares together and machine- or hand-quilt through all layers with white thread.

5. Join the squares with slip stitch as described in Basic Techniques, p. 14.

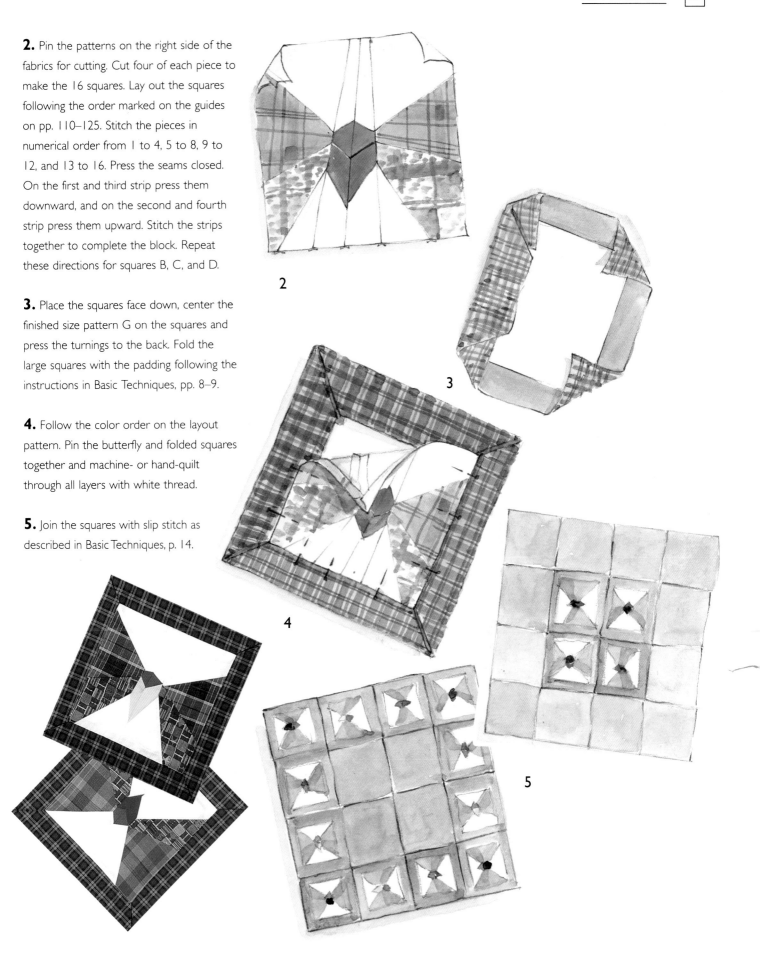

2

3

4

5

Butterflies color charts
front (above), back (below)

French Tiles

◆■◆■◆■◆■◆■◆■◆■◆■◆■◆■◆■◆■◆■◆■◆■◆■◆■■

THE INSPIRATION FOR THIS QUILT CAME FROM SOME ANCIENT FRENCH TILES, INTERPRETED IN THE COLORS OF AFRICAN TEXTILES. IT IS A COMBINATION OF SQUARES FOLDED INTO SQUARES AND CIRCLES FOLDED INTO SQUARES. THE LARGE SQUARES AND CIRCLES ARE MADE WITH HAND DYED FABRICS, SOME BOUGHT AND SOME DYED WITH THE COLORS RUNNING INTO EACH OTHER. THIS IS DONE BY FOLLOWING THE INSTRUCTIONS ON THE PACKETS OF THE DYES. DIP A BIT OF THE FABRIC INTO THE DYE, LEAVE IT IN THE BOWL AND LET IT RUN UP AND DOWN ONTO THE NEXT SPACE TO BE DYED.

FINISHED QUILT SIZE: 50 × 70 INCHES

YOU WILL NEED

Materials
- ◆ plain fabric to be dyed in strips, 79 × 36 in.
- ◆ hand-dyed cotton, 40 × 48 in. each
- ◆ rust, red, orange, light and dark turquoise, and dark green African textiles, 91 × 18 in.
- ◆ variation of six patterns—alternatively use any abstract, brightly colored fabrics or scraps
- ◆ dyes—brown, rust, green, yellow, and turquoise
- ◆ cotton flannel sheet for padding, single bed size
- ◆ sewing thread, beige and dark brown

Pattern Guides
- ● A 10½ in. diameter circle
- ● B 10 in. diameter circle
- ● C 9 in. square
- ● D 7 in. square
- ● E 6 in. square
- ● F 5½ in. square

Number of square pieces to cut
Side One
- ■ A nine × light and dark turquoise
- ■ C nine × mixed colors
- ■ D nine × patterned fabrics
- ■ E nine × patterned fabrics

Side Two
- ■ C 36 × mixed colors
  - 10 × light and dark turquoise
  - 10 × hand-dyed mixed colors
  - seven × dark brown
  - three × dark green
  - one × yellow
  - two × red
  - 21 × mixed colors (for triangles on borders)
- ■ D 54 × cotton flannel padding
  - 11 × cotton flannel to be cut in half for triangles
- ■ E 36 × patterned fabrics

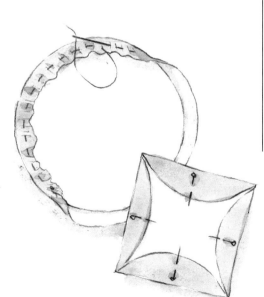

1. Gather the fabric circles over the paper patterns and proceed to fold into squares following the instructions in Basic Techniques, pp. 10–11. Insert the padding and squares cut from pattern D into the folded circles and pin.

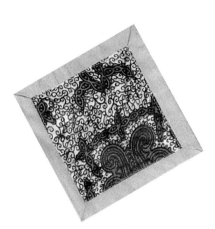

3. Machine quilt the layered pieces, starting and ending on one of the flat sides and overlapping three or four stitches, leaving about 6 in. long thread ends. Do not start at the points, as it is too hard to match the join of the stitches. When finished, pull the threads through to one side and stitch the ends between the layers.

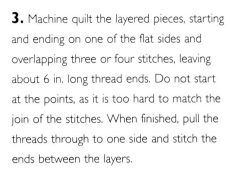

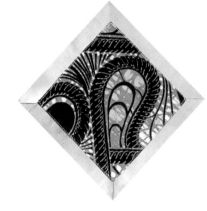

2. Fold the large squares into squares following the instructions in Basic Techniques, pp. 8–9. To fold the small squares, fold the turnings to the back using pattern E, place them over the edges of the large squares and pin in place.

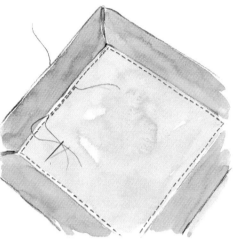

French Tiles color charts
front (left), back (right)

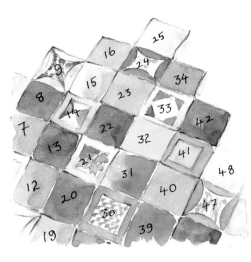

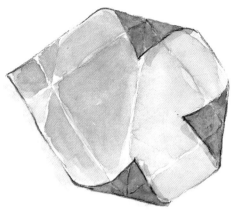

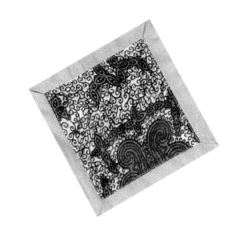

4. Lay out side one first with the squares on the points. The circles and squares are in columns 2, 5, and 8. When this side is complete, move any odd squares around to get an all-over pattern. Turn the squares over to see the other side. Some of the squares may need to be turned or moved depending upon the patterned fabric designs and colors. When you are satisfied with the design, number all the pieces in diagonal strips with small, sticky dots placed at the top point of each square, starting from top left and progressing to bottom right.

6. The border is made of 21 squares of mixed colors and triangular shaped half squares of padding. Fold the squares to the finished size using pattern D.

8. Then fold the unpadded half of the square up to make a right-angled triangle. Ladder stitch the two folded edges closed.

7. Place the padding in half of the square under the turning allowance. Refold the pointed corners in, as for a mitered corner.

5. Starting with 2, 3, and 4 pick up the pieces in nine strips in numerical order, which will keep the squares in the correct order for stitching. Stitch them together with ladder stitch.

9. Place these triangles around the quilt following the layout design. Stitch together with ladder stitch.

Antique Flowers

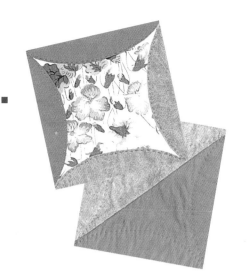

THE PRINTED FLOWERS IN THE CIRCLES WERE GIVEN TO THE QUILTMAKER BY AN ELDERLY LADY WHO KNEW THE FABRIC FROM HER CHILDHOOD. THE PIECES, WHICH ORIGINALLY HAD A VICTORIAN RED AND WHITE POLKA DOT BORDER PRINTED ON THEM, WERE TOO DELICATE TO BE USED ON THEIR OWN TO MAKE A PATCHWORK. THE FOLDED PATCHWORK TECHNIQUE HAS ALLOWED THE LOVELY SQUARES TO BE USED SAFELY BY FRAMING THEM IN CIRCLES OF NEW FABRIC.

FINISHED QUILT SIZE: 64 INCHES SQUARE

YOU WILL NEED

Materials

- ◆ plain dark mauve 48 × 48 in.
- ◆ plain light mauve 60 × 48 in.
- ◆ patterned yellow-green 20 × 45 in.
- ◆ plain turquoise 60 × 48 in.
- ◆ small dark checks 84 × 48 in.
- ◆ tan flower pattern 98 × 48 in.
- ◆ tan dotted print 60 × 48 in.
- ◆ 20 antique squares 8 × 8 in.
- ◆ cotton flannel padding—one single bed sheet

Pattern Guides

- ● A 12½ in. diameter half circle
- ● B 11½ in. diameter circle
- ● C 8 in. square to be cut in half diagonally
- ● D 14 × 14 × 20½ in.
- ● E 7 in. square
- ● F 6 in. square

Number of pieces to cut

- ■ A 12 × plain green and
  12 × dark mauve
  20 × light mauve and
  20 × turquoise
- ■ C 12 × dark mauve and
  12 × dotted tan
  12 × dark mauve and
  12 × tan flower print
  eight × tan flower print and
  eight × dotted tan
- ■ D 20 × antique squares
  12 × dotted tan
  64 × cotton flannel padding
- ■ E 32 × dark checks

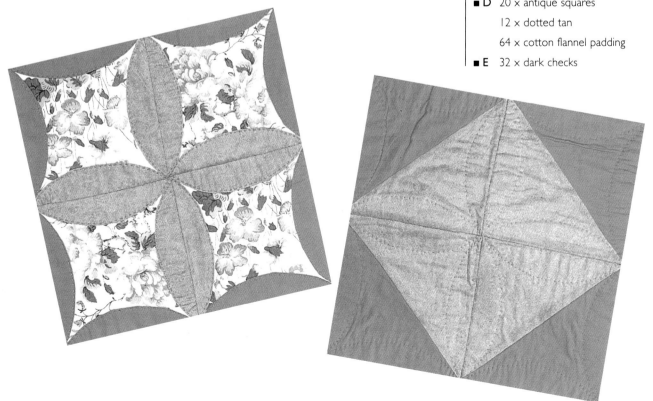

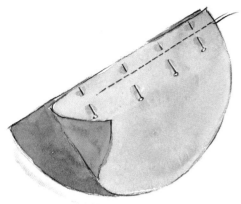

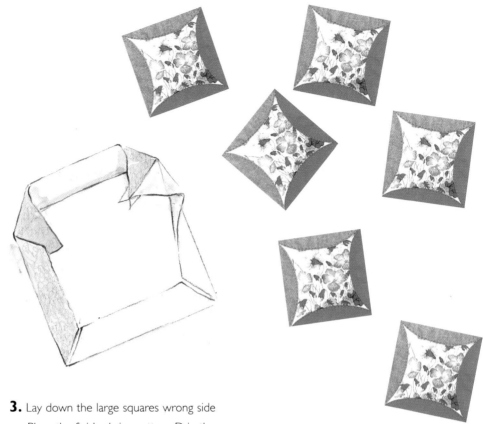

1. The half circles and triangles that are listed in pairs for cutting are to be stitched together along the seam line of the patterns. Press the seams closed and to one side of the pieces. Begin by gathering the circles with a running stitch around the outside edges on the right side. Place the paper pattern B, in the center, on the wrong side of the fabric. Pull both ends of the gathering thread until the fabric is gathered over the paper, tie a knot in the thread and press under the edges of the fabric.

3. Lay down the large squares wrong side up. Place the finished size pattern D in the center, fold the edges to the back and press. Remove the pattern, insert the padding, fold the corners in and then the sides as described in Basic Techniques, pp. 8–9.

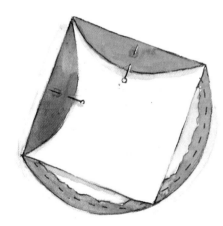

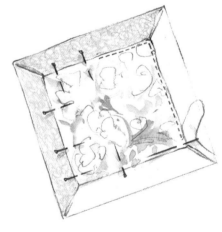

2. Remove the paper pattern and fold the circles into squares following the instructions in Basic Techniques, pp.8–9 for circles into squares. Place the antique squares in the turquoise and light mauve circles and the dotted tan squares in the dark mauve and green circles. Baste ready for quilting.

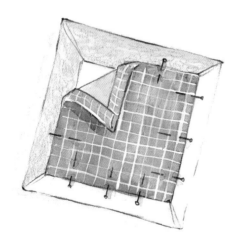

4. Fold the dark checked small squares over the finished size pattern, press, remove pattern and place in the center of the large squares.

5. Matching the points to the mitered corners, pin in place and baste the small squares ready for quilting. Hand quilt the folded edges with a running stitch going through all the layers. Start to stitch on the folded edge, and not on the points, because this will make it easier to start and finish the quilting threads between the layers. Join the squares together using ladder stitch.

6. Join the squares in blocks of four. There are five antique flower blocks—gather the center on the light mauve points and ladder stitch the edges together as described in Basic Techniques, p.14. The squares to be gathered are on the seamed corners in the center. Following the design layout going clockwise they are:

- dark mauve and tan flower square
- to dotted tan and tan flower square
- to dotted tan and tan flower square
- to dotted tan and dark mauve square

7. Join the large blocks with the squares facing one way and the circles the other, following the layout design, with the dark mauve fabric facing out. Finally add the border pieces by joining them in three pairs with the corners.

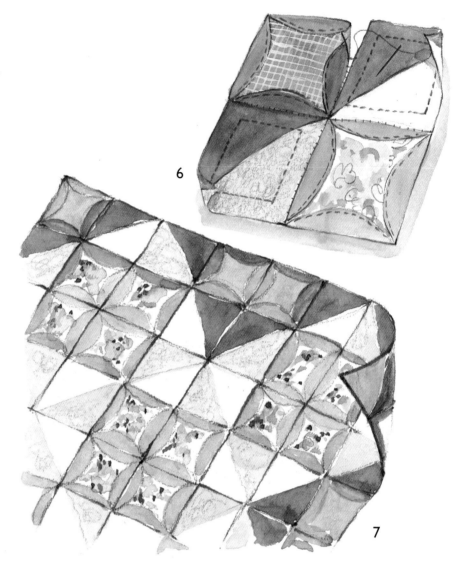

6

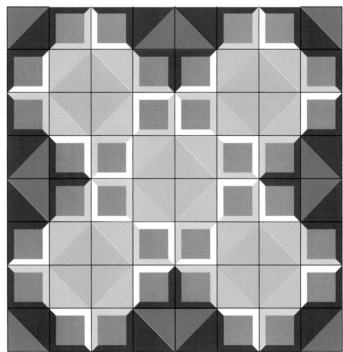

7

Antique Flowers color charts
front (left), back (right)

Anemones de Caen

◆■□◆■□◆■□◆■□◆■□◆■□◆■□◆■□◆■□◆■□◆■□◆■□◆■□◆■□◆■□◆

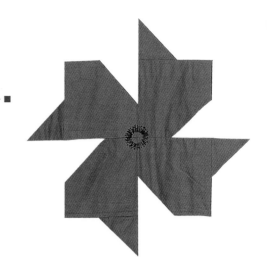

THE BRIGHTLY COLORED FLOWERS OF ANEMONES ARE THE INSPIRATION FOR THIS QUILT. THE FLOWERS STAND OUT WELL AGAINST THE BLACK BACKGROUND. THE FOLDED SIDE IS VERY DIFFERENT IN MOOD FROM THE FLOWERS, ALLOWING YOU TO SET A DIFFERENT SCENE IN THE BEDROOM SIMPLY BY TURNING THE QUILT OVER.

FINISHED QUILT SIZE: 90 × 81 INCHES

YOU WILL NEED

Materials

◆ plain colored cotton:

1. red 69 × 48 in.

2. light pink 29½ × 48 in.

3. purple 29½ × 48 in.

4. light purple 69 × 48 in.

5. magenta 69 × 48 in.

6. light magenta 29½ × 48 in.

7. red/pink 29½ × 48 in.

8. cream 29½ × 48 in.

9. black 7½ yd × 48 in.

batik print 79 × 48 in.

pink and black 79 × 48 in.

◆ cotton flannel padding—one double-bed sized sheet

◆ black stranded embroidery cotton

◆ black sewing and quilting threads

Pattern Guides

● A 13 in. square

● B 10 in. square, to be cut in half diagonally for triangles on the squares

● C 9 in. square

● D 8 in. square

● E 7 in. square

Number of pieces to cut

■ A eight × color 1, four × color 2, four × color 3, eight × color 4, eight × color 5, four × color 6, four × color 7, four × color 8 and 44 × color 9
29 of color 9 for solid squares

■ B 10 × color 1, two × color 2, two × color 3, two × color 4, four × color 5, two × color 6, two × color 7, two × color 8 and nine × color 9

■ C 90 × cotton flannel padding

■ D 44 × batik printed cotton
46 × pink and black printed cotton

1. Piece the squares with the triangles by placing the right sides together matching the seam line to the mark on the pattern at 4½ in. from the corner. Stitch by machine or hand with a running stitch. Trim the excess fabric and press the seams closed.

2. Place pattern C in the center of the wrong side of the large square and fold following the Basic Techniques, pp.10–11 for the folded squares.

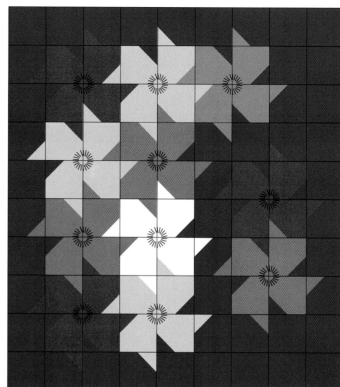

Anemones de Caen color charts
front (left), back (right)

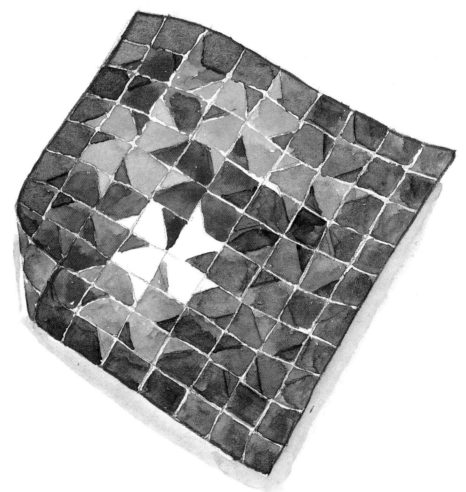

3. For the placement of the small squares, follow the overall design by laying out all the squares, anemone side up and numbering them with sticky dots placed on the top left hand corner of each square. Pick the squares up in rows and stack them ready for the small squares. The large squares to have the pink and black printed small squares added have numbers: 1 to 10 inclusive and 11, 20, 21, 30, 31, 40, 41, 50, 51, 52, 53, 55, 56, 57, 60, 61, 67, 70, 71, 72, 77, 78, 79, 80, 81 to 90 inclusive. All the remaining squares use the batik printed squares.

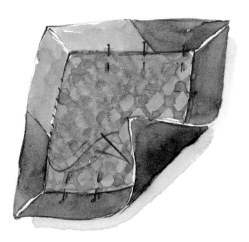

4. Ladder stitch into the folded edges of the small square and then through the front of the large square and the padding only. Do not go through to the other side with the stitches.

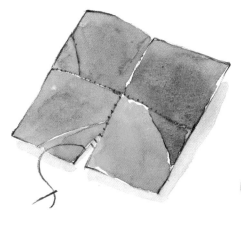

5. Lay out all the pieces again in numerical order and ladder stitch them together in pairs and blocks as described in Basic Techniques, p.14.

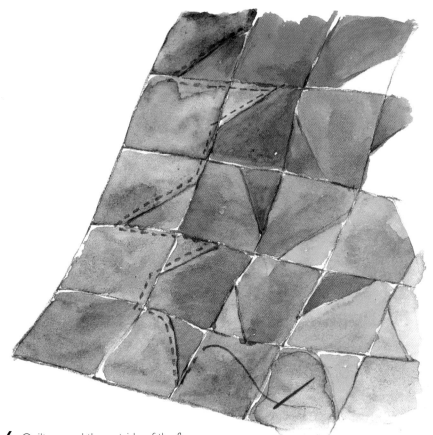

6. Quilt around the outside of the flowers about ¼ in. from the seam lines with black quilting thread.

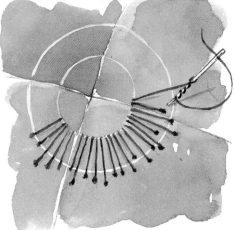

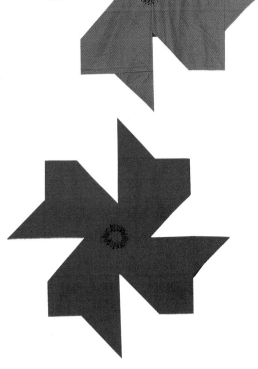

7. Embroider the flower centers with french knots on stems. Draw a double ring over the join in the center of the flowers with tailors' chalk. Make the stitches with three strands of the black stranded cotton. Take the needle between the layers and start on the inner circle, placing the knots on and below the outer ring. This will give a staggered, natural effect.

Circus Cot Quilt

THE COT QUILT IS MADE OF PIECED CIRCLES FOLDED INTO SQUARES TO FORM THE BORDER OF A LARGE RECTANGLE IN THE CENTER. THE INSIDE OF THE CIRCLES HAVE BEEN PAINTED ON BY THE QUILTMAKER WITH FABRIC PAINTS AND A BLACK WATERPROOF OUTLINE PEN. IF YOU WANT TO HAVE A GO, THERE ARE FABRIC PAINTS, PENS, AND CRAYONS IN CRAFT SHOPS, BUT REMEMBER TO FOLLOW THE DIRECTIONS CAREFULLY. FOR THE DESIGNS, YOU CAN USE SHAPES IN OLD-FASHIONED COLORING BOOKS. SIMPLY PLACE THE WHITE FABRIC SQUARES OVER THE FIGURES AND TRACE THEM ONTO THE FABRIC WITH A SOFT PENCIL. YOU CAN THEN ADD COLOR TO THESE, ALTHOUGH IT IS A GOOD IDEA TO DO A FEW TEST SAMPLES FIRST. ALTERNATIVELY THERE ARE SOME PRINTED FABRICS IN THE SHOPS WITH CIRCUS MOTIFS ON THEM.

FINISHED QUILT SIZE: 30 x 36 INCHES

YOU WILL NEED

Materials

◆ plain cotton fabrics, 18 x 48 in. (yellow, blue, green, and white)
◆ red and white stripe, 36 x 48 in.
◆ cotton flannel padding, 36 x 40 in.
◆ green bias tape
◆ white quilting thread

Pattern Guides

● A 9 in. diameter half circles
● B 9 in. diameter quarter circle
● C 8½ in. diameter gathering circle
● D 6 in. square
● E 28 x 22 in. rectangle
● F 24 x 18 in. rectangle
● G 22 x 16 in. rectangle

Number of pieces to cut

■ A 14 x blue half circles
    seven x red and white striped half circles for right-hand side
    eight x red and white striped half circles for left-hand side and centre top
    three x green half circles
■ B three x yellow quarter circles
    three x green quarter circles
    one x red and white striped quarter circles
    one x blue quarter circle
■ D 18 x squares of padding and circus figures each
■ E one x yellow rectangle
■ F one x rectangle of padding and red and white stripe each

1. When cutting the circles that are striped, make sure the right side of the fabric is facing up, so that you can match the direction of the stripes to the pattern. This applies to the quarter circle as well. Pin the pieces together along the stitch line and sew by machine or hand with a running stitch. Press the seams closed and to one side of the circles.

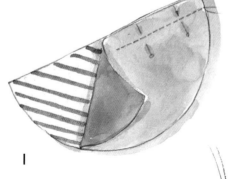

2. Piece the remaining four circles by joining the two quarter circles together to make a half circle, the stripe with the blue and the yellow with the green. Press the seams closed and join these to the other half circles to make the full circles.

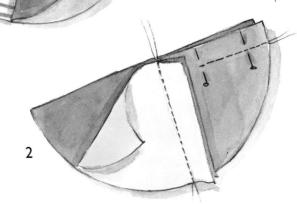

3. Gather the circles over paper and press, following the instructions in Basic Techniques, pp.10–11 for circles folded into squares. When placing pattern C on the wrong side of the circles, match the corners of the square with the seam lines and then fold and press. Remove the paper, insert the padding and inside squares and refold. Pin in place ready for quilting.

4

5

6

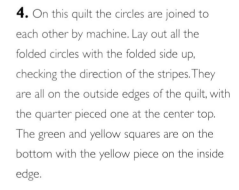

4. On this quilt the circles are joined to each other by machine. Lay out all the folded circles with the folded side up, checking the direction of the stripes. They are all on the outside edges of the quilt, with the quarter pieced one at the center top. The green and yellow squares are on the bottom with the yellow piece on the inside edge.

5. Stitch the pieces to each other by picking them up in pairs, unpinning and unfolding the flaps. Stitch by machine or hand with a running stitch along the wrong side of the fold lines. Finish the ends with an additional backstitch by hand, refold the flaps and pin in place.

6. Join the three top and bottom pieces and stitch along both sides to make four strips.

7. Next join the top and bottom strips to the large yellow rectangle. Mark the large piece to the finished size on the right side of the fabric. Place the top strip folds along the marked line, unpin, open the flaps, and pin in place. Stitch along the folded lines on the inside of the circles, finishing off both ends with a backstitch. Repeat this for the bottom and both sides. Stitch the four corners separately by hand with a ladder stitch. Baste around all the folded edges.

8. Lay the quilt out with the center side up. Insert the padding and fold the corners and flaps the same way that a square is folded, as described in Basic Techniques, pp. 8–9. Fold the edges of the inner rectangle to the finished size and place over the large rectangle, matching the points with the mitred corners. Pin in place and baste all the edges.

Circus Cot Quilt color charts
front (left), back (right)

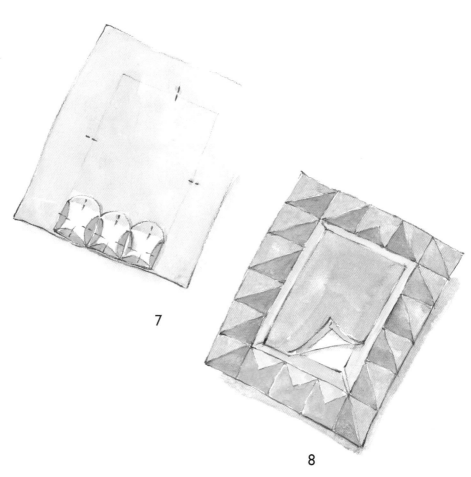

7

8

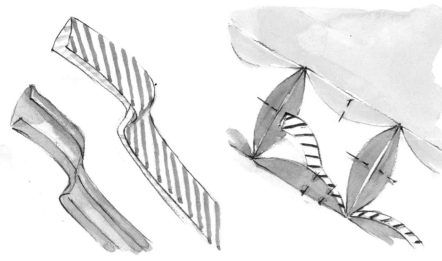

9. Make striped bias tape by cutting two lengths, an inch wide, of the striped fabric at a right-angle from the selvage edge. Join the pieces. Fold in half lengthwise and press the crease. The plain green bias is made with a double-folded edge.

10. Cut three 6 in. pieces of the striped bias and slip them just under the edges of the circles on the three bottom squares. Tuck the raw ends under the edges and quilt in place.

11. Quilt around all the squares and the rectangle with white quilting thread using a running stitch through all the layers.

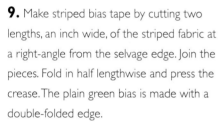

12. From the pattern, mark on the finished size rectangle the inside line of the green circle. It should be 13 in. in diameter. Pin the inside edge of the green bias tape to the marked circle and baste in place. Pin the outside edge of the tape and then slip the striped bias under this edge, unpinning and repinning as you go. Overlap the ends and fold the top one back under itself. Baste in place and quilt both edges of the green bias tape. Mark the tent shape, with tailors' chalk, on the inside of the ring and quilt.

Green Flower Throwover

This throwover was made to be used on the back of a rocking chair for excluding draughts and giving comfort and warmth in the winter. The use of circles folded into squares gives this quilt a flower on one side and diamond shape on the other. By placing the light-colored squares in the center of the circles and quilting the flower shape on it, the quilt is like the old-fashioned summer and winter quilts of the Amish. The addition of a border is also a special feature of this quilt.

Finished quilt size: 30 x 42 inches

YOU WILL NEED

Materials
- plain beige cotton, 24 x 48 in.
- plain dark green, 40 x 48 in.
- printed light green, 20 x 48 in.
- printed dark green, 30 x 48 in.
- padding, 36 x 45 in.
- dark green quilting thread

Pattern Guides
- A 6½ in. diameter half circle
- B 5½ in. diameter circle
- C 4 in. square
- D template for quilting

Number of pieces to cut
Cut four 1 x 48 in. strips for the outside borders on the printed dark green fabric before cutting the half circles
- A 54 x light and dark green printed fabrics
- C 54 x padding and beige fabric
  Cut four 3 x 48 in. strips for the inside border of the plain dark green fabric
  Four 2½ x 45 in. strips of padding

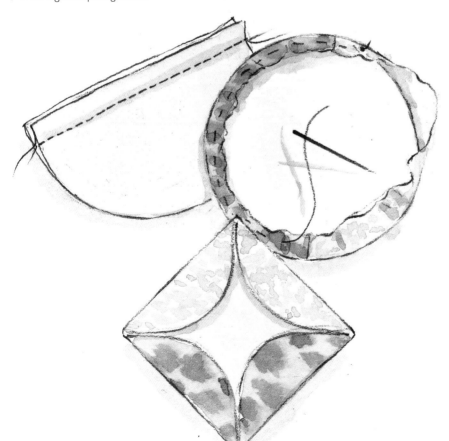

1. Join the two shades of the green half circles by machine or hand using a running stitch, along the stitch line. Gather the circles on the paper pattern B, press, remove the paper and fold the circles into squares by following the instructions in Basic Techniques, pp. 8–9. Make sure the seams of the circles are on two points of the pattern. Insert the padding and the squares of beige in each folded circle, pin and quilt around the folded edges with the dark green quilting thread. At the same time quilt the center of the squares using the template on page 126.

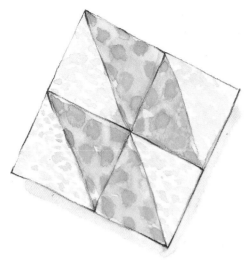

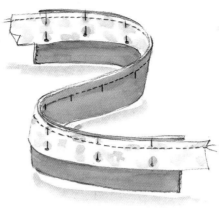

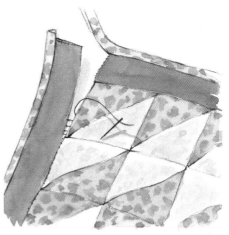

2. Lay the pieces out on the diamond side to see the whole pattern. Join the squares in groups of four. Gather the points of the squares and ladder stitch them following the instructions in Basic Techniques, p.14.

4. Take a printed dark green strip, 36 in. long. With right sides facing, pin the long sides together and stitch the strips ¼ in. from the outside edges of the dark green strip. Turn the two ends of the printed green strip and fold it back on itself. Fold the turning allowance over the raw edges on the two long sides and ladder stitch. Leave the ends open to be turned in when borders are added to the quilt. The remaining two pieces of green fabric are cut 36 in. long, and the printed strip 37 in. long. Cut the padding 35 in. long. Fold lengthwise, press and stitch in the same way as the shorter pieces.

6. Stitch the remaining two green, folded edges to the long sides, including the ends of the 24 in. borders. Fold the printed green border over the raw edges and ends of the 36 in. length of plain green border. Turn under and ladder stitch down the length of the short side.

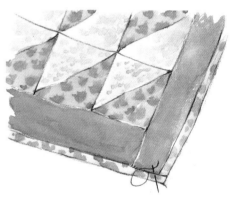

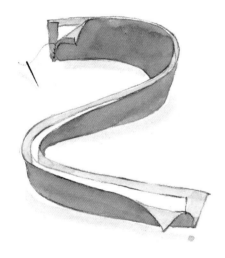

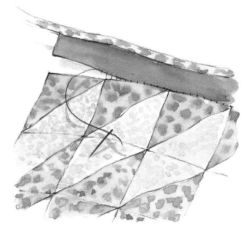

3. On two of the plain, dark green strips of fabric to be used for the borders, cut 26 in. lengths, fold them in half lengthwise and press in a crease. Unfold the pieces and lay 24 in. lengths of padding inside the fabric along the crease line. Fold the cut ends over the padding, refold the fabric and pin the raw edges together.

5. Attach the 24 in. borders to the quilt with ladder stitch: pin the crease line of the dark green to the edges of the squares. Stitch the folded ends of the border at the same time.

7. Hem the printed borders on the short sides, trim the excess off, and fold the ends to enclose the raw edges of the long side. Ladder stitch all edges closed.

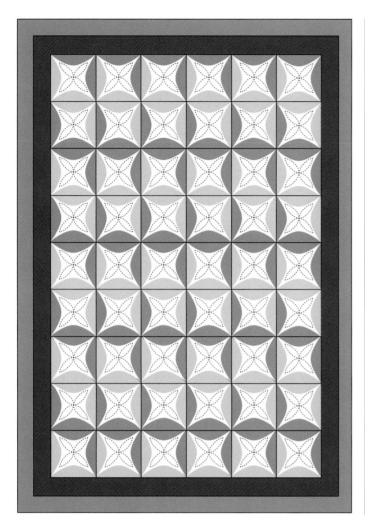

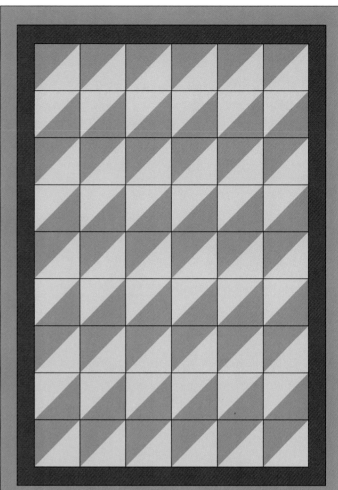

Green Flower Throwover color charts
front (above left), back (above right)

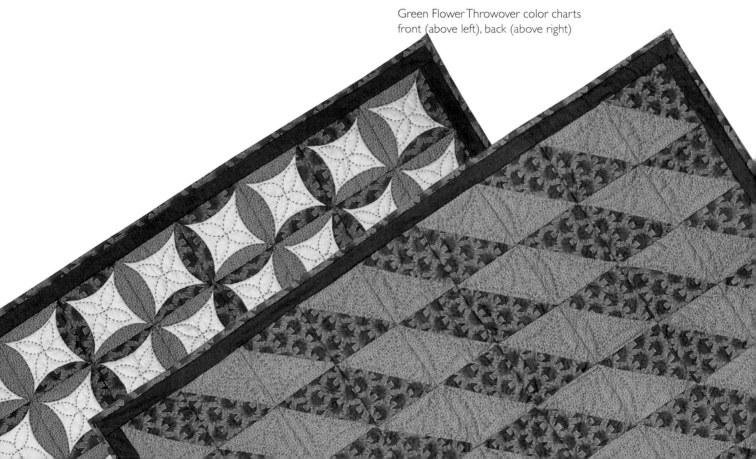

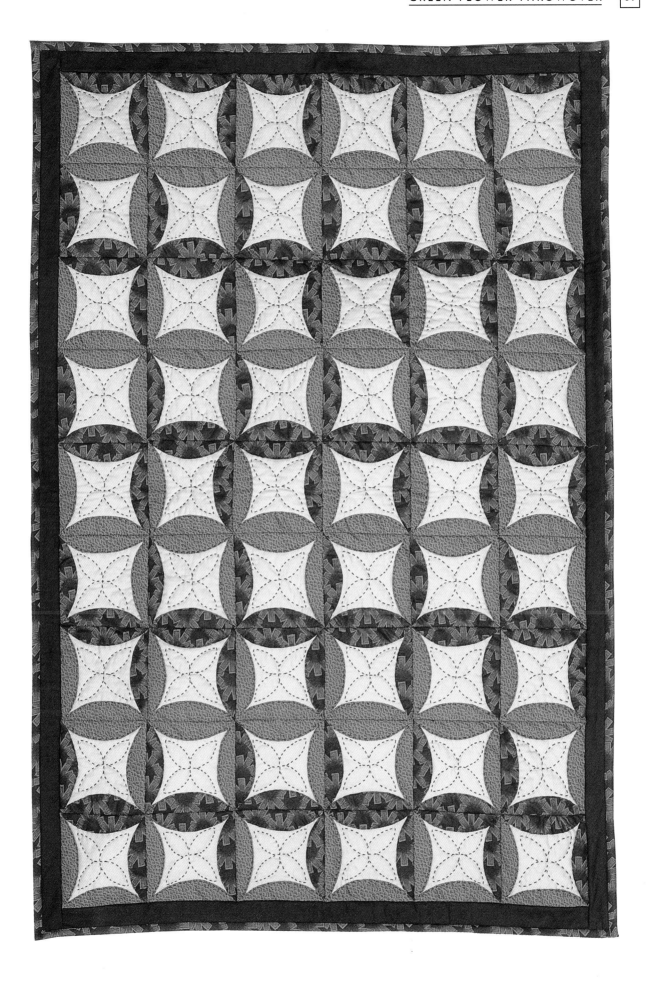

Hexagon Star

◆■●◆■●◆■●◆■●◆■●◆■●◆■●◆■●◆■●◆■●◆■●◆■●◆■●◆■●◆■●◆■●◆

This mat can be used as a basket liner, a cover on a bread basket, or as a table mat for Christmas dinner. It can also be made larger and used as a cot quilt, a throwover on a chair, or even a full-sized quilt. It is made by putting a hexagon on the point inside a larger folded hexagon.

Finished size: 13 inches in diameter

YOU WILL NEED

Materials
◆ printed cottons 18 × 18 in. or fat quarters of three greens, and one white
◆ cotton flannel padding 20 × 20 in.
◆ white quilting thread

Pattern Guides
● A   hexagon, each side 3½ in.
● B   hexagon, each side 3 in.
● C   hexagon, each side 2¾ in.

Number of pieces to cut
■ A   one × light green hexagon from scrap
   three each of the two green fabrics
■ C   seven × white inner hexagons
   seven × padding hexagons

2. Remove the paper and insert the padding and inner hexagon with their points halfway along the straight sides of the larger hexagon. Fold the points over the edges of the inner hexagons and pin the points in place. The outside corners will overlap slightly, covering the points of the inner shapes.

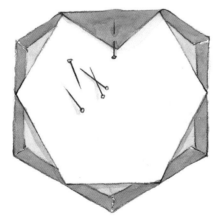

1. Place the large hexagons face down, center pattern B and press the turning allowance to the back. Baste the points of the turnings with a backstitch to hold the shape. Do not stitch through the paper.

3. Quilt around the pieces, starting on a flat side of the hexagon and not on a point. This makes it easier to start and finish the ends of the quilting threads.

4. Arrange the hexagonal pieces to form the desired shape.

5. Join the hexagons with a ladder stitch along the folded edges, making an additional backstitch at all the points.

Hexagon Star color charts front (above), back (below)

Hexagon Bag

◆■◆■◆■◆■◆■◆■◆■◆■◆■◆■◆■◆■◆■◆■◆■◆■

This decorative bag is made of hexagons folded with smaller hexagons in the center. The bag is double-sided with small peach hexagons for top and bottom rows and red for the middle row on the other side. The base of the bag is made of one large, double-sided hexagon.

Finished size: 10½ x 24 inches

YOU WILL NEED

Materials
- ◆ Three pieces of printed cotton (purple, purple and red, gray, and pink), 18 × 18 in. square or fat quarters
- ◆ chintz pink and red, 6 × 48 in. or scraps
- ◆ gray bias tape, 12 in. long
- ◆ braid for ties, 36 in.
- ◆ cotton flannel padding, 18 × 36 in.

Pattern Guides
See templates on p.126 for pattern guides
- ● A cut size for large hexagon
- ● B finished size for large hexagon
- ● C cut size for small hexagon
- ● D finished size for small hexagon
- ● E cut size for base
- ● F finished size for base

Number of pieces to cut
- ■ A six × each of the printed fabrics
- ■ B 18 × padding
- ■ C six × peach chintz
  12 × red chintz
- ■ D 18 × paper
- ■ E one × same fabric as the middle row
  one × same fabric as the bottom row
- ■ F one × padding

1. Fold a length of bias tape in half lengthwise and machine stitch the folded edges together. Cut into six equal lengths for the loops. Assemble the large and small hexagons following Basic Techniques pp.12–13. Quilt the layers with cream quilting thread. Do not complete the last six patches.

2. On the top row of hexagons insert the raw ends of the bias tape loops before quilting. After quilting finish off by oversewing the loop and the hexagon.

3. Join each row of hexagons with ladder stitch and using a backstitch at the points. Join two rows together using ladder stitch.

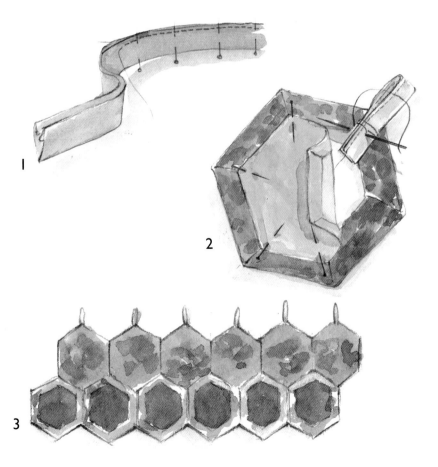

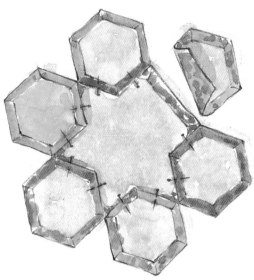

5. Turn the bag inside out and ladder stitch the base to the hexagons.

7. Cut the length of the braid in two, thread one piece through the loops and tie the two ends together with a knot about 4 in. from the cut ends. Thread the second piece through the loops starting from the middle of the first braid and tie a knot in both ends. Unravel the ends of the braids and cut the ends to the desired length.

4. Make the hexagon base by marking the finished size lines on the wrong side of one of the fabrics. Place the two printed pieces, right sides together and stitch by machine around five of the sides of the hexagons. Place the padding on the wrong side and turn the whole shape right side out. Push all the points out and fold the turning allowance of the sixth side in to be ladder stitched closed. While the bag is still flat, pin the points of the single row of hexagons to the base, folding the points over the sides of the base. Pin the points in place and ladder stitch the edges to the hexagon base making a star shape.

6. To finish off, stitch the remaining two rows to the base and stitch the two open sides together to complete the bag.

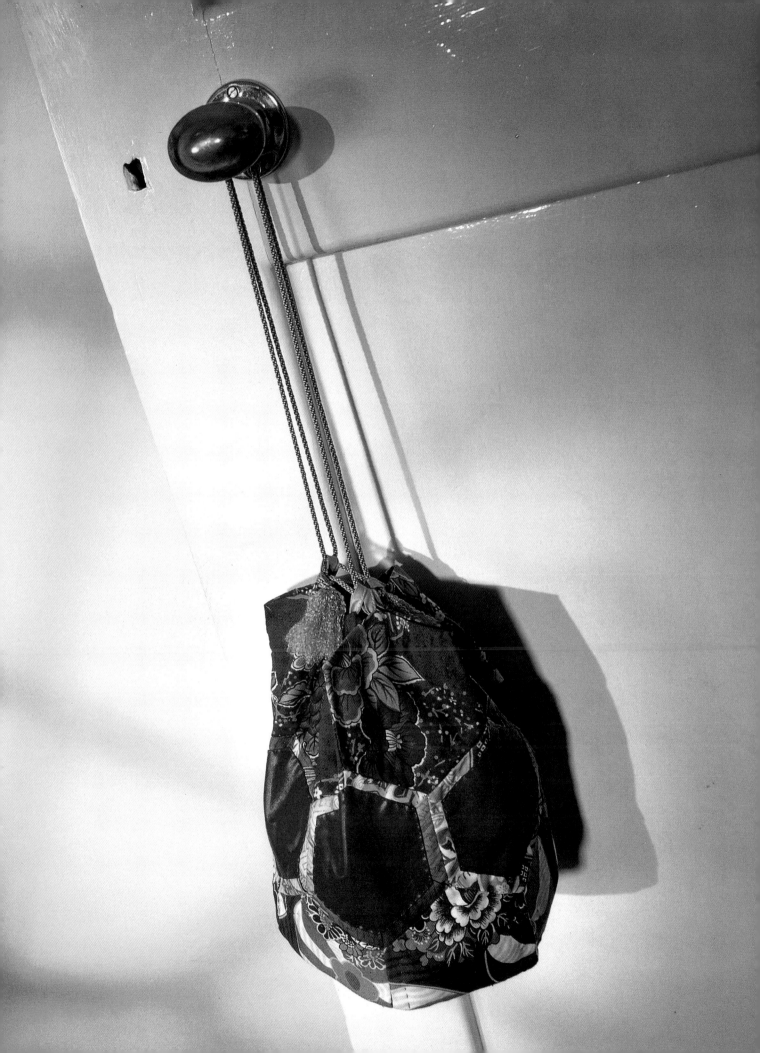

Indian Bedspread

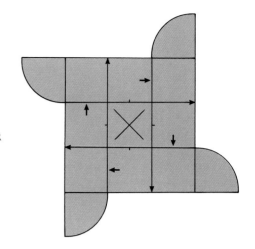

THE BEDSPREAD IS MADE OF A PRINTED CLOTH FROM INDIA THAT HAS THE PATTERNED CENTER TAKEN OUT. THE BORDER PATTERN HAS BEEN SEWN ONTO A FLANNEL SHEET AND A PLAIN WHITE FABRIC CENTER HAS BEEN ADDED. THE CENTER WAS THEN QUILTED IN THE JAPANESE SASHIKO STYLE WITH THREE SHADES OF BLUE QUILTING THREAD. BECAUSE THERE ARE ONLY TWO LAYERS, THE BEDSPREAD IS SUITABLE FOR LIGHTWEIGHT SUMMER USE. IT IS ALSO USEFUL AS A COVER OVER A DUVET BECAUSE THE FLANNEL SHEETING WILL HELP TO KEEP IT FROM SLIPPING OFF. THE PATTERNED CENTER THAT HAS BEEN CUT OUT CAN BE USED TO MAKE MATCHING CUSHION COVERS, PILLOW CASES, OR BORDERS ON CURTAINS.

FINISHED QUILT SIZE: DOUBLE BED SIZE

YOU WILL NEED

Materials

- ◆ one bedspread from India, double bed sized
- ◆ one cotton flannel sheet, double bed sized
- ◆ plain white cotton, 4½ yd × 36 in.
- ◆ three shades of blue quilting thread

Templates

Make the template for the quilting shape by tracing the pattern on p.127 onto paper or photocopying it. Paste it onto lightweight card and cut the shape out, including the center square.

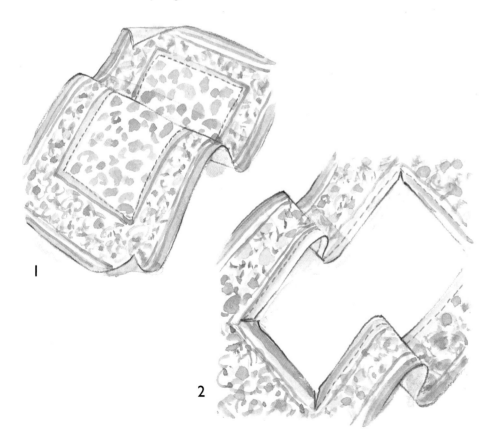

1

2

1. Unpick any stitched edges on the bedspread and sheet. Press the creases out on both. Machine stitch the bedspread around the inside edge of the border that is to be turned under. This will help to keep the turnings straight and reinforce the corners.

2. Cut out the center of the bedspread about an inch from the stitched line. Clip into the corners up to the stitches.

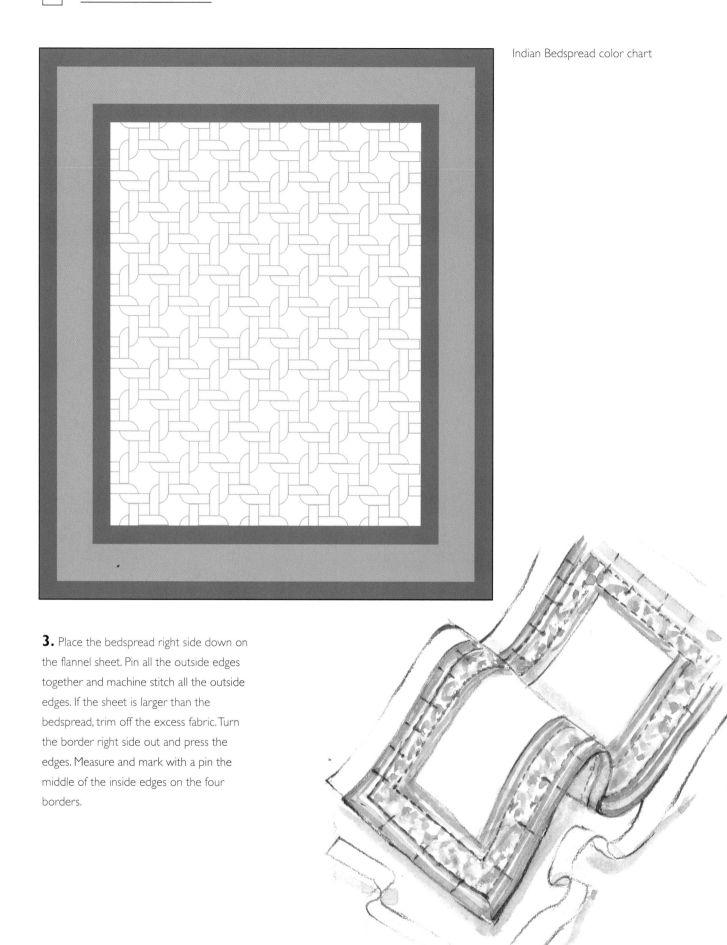

Indian Bedspread color chart

3. Place the bedspread right side down on the flannel sheet. Pin all the outside edges together and machine stitch all the outside edges. If the sheet is larger than the bedspread, trim off the excess fabric. Turn the border right side out and press the edges. Measure and mark with a pin the middle of the inside edges on the four borders.

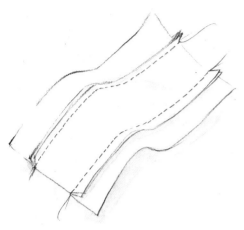

4. Mark the center piece by cutting two equal lengths, one of which will be the middle panel. The second is cut down the length to the width required to make the panel plus 4 in. Remove all the selvages before stitching because they may pucker when they are washed. Stitch both of these pieces to either side of the middle piece by machine. Press the seams closed and to one side of the panel, either both facing into the middle or out to the sides.

5. Fold this piece in half lengthwise and crosswise and press. Place this piece on the center of the bedspread and match the creases to the pins marking the middle of the borders. Slip the center under the edges of the border, turn the edges, pin and baste around the four sides.

6. Baste across the center creases in both directions. Mark for quilting starting from the crossed center lines. Mark the pattern for quilting the whole center before starting to stitch. Place the template on the center, with the basted line running through the middle of the square hole. Using tailors' chalk or chalk pencil, mark around the outside of the template as well as the center square. Lift the template off and make the additional lines extending from the center square out to the curved lines. Move the template over and down to meet the straight inside lines for the next pattern. Repeat until the whole piece has been marked out.

7. Quilt four center shapes that make the twist in the middle with the darkest blue thread. This will make a diamond of color. Use the medium shade of blue for the next row of twists out from the center. Make the remaining twists with the lightest shade of blue. Quilt in the Japanese Sashiko style using a heavy thread and running stitch. Starting and ending with the threads, run between the layers making two small backstitches along the lines to be quilted over. Start quilting from the center out.

8. To finish the quilt, stitch around the borders along the folded edges to hold all the layers together. You may also wish to quilt along the lines of the printed borders, as this will give the bedspread more body and finish it off well.

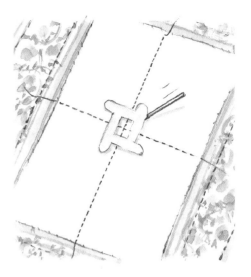

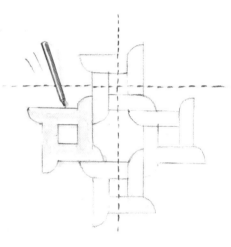

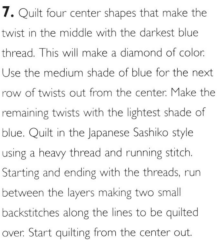

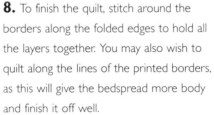

Indian Cushion Covers

THIS IS A QUICK AND EASY WAY TO MAKE COVERS FOR CUSHIONS TO MATCH THE INDIAN BEDSPREAD. THEY ARE VERY USEFUL BECAUSE YOU CAN SLIP THEM OVER CUSHIONS THAT MAY ALREADY BE COVERED, TO MATCH A WINTER QUILT, OR YOU MAY JUST WANT A CHANGE EVERY SO OFTEN. FOR ONE OF THE COVERS I USED SOME OF THE FABRIC THAT WAS IN THE CENTER OF THE ORIGINAL BEDSPREAD. THE OTHER COMES FROM SOME SOFT, STRIPED SHIRTING FABRIC.

FINISHED SIZE OF CUSHION COVERS: 14 INCHES SQUARE

YOU WILL NEED

Materials
◆ Blue and white stripe, 18 × 48 in.
◆ Printed cotton, 18 × 18 in.
◆ Plain white cotton, 18 × 18 in.
◆ Two packets of bias tape, one white and one blue
◆ Two cushion pads, 14 in. or 15 in. square

Pattern Guides
Make paper pattern guides for the cut fabric size, to be scaled up to full size (see template on p.127)
● A Back and triangles to be tied on the front
● B Inside front—16 × 15 in. rectangle

Number of pieces to cut
■ One × both pattern guides for each cushion

1. Cut out the fabric pieces, using patterns A and B.

2. Open the bias tape edge and match it to the wrong side of one of the fabric edges, proceeding outwards to the point of the triangle. Pin in place. Leave some tape at end to be turned under later. Stitch by machine along the crease line of the bias tape to the point. With the needle left down in the point of the fabrics, lift the foot and turn the triangle and the bias tape 45 degrees. Pin the tape to the other edge, moving the extra tape from under the foot, replace the foot and stitch the pieces together to the end. Cut the bias tape with a turning allowance.

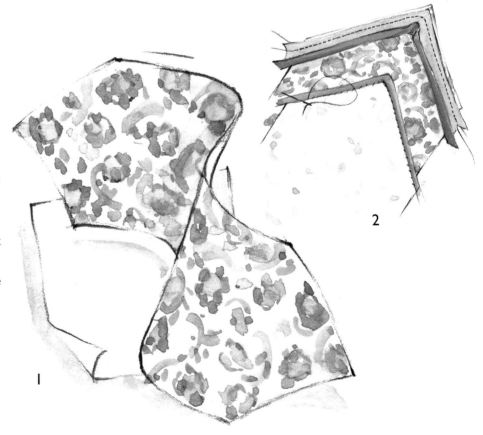

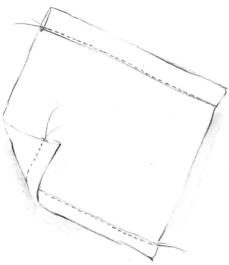

4. Place the wrong sides of the fabrics together, pin along the raw edges and machine stitch ¼ in. from the edges. Press the seams, turn the pieces inside out with ight sides together and press the folded edges. Pin both the edges and stitch a seam line with a generous ¼ in. allowance. Press and turn inside out again. This gives a double turned seam that has no raw edges to fray.

3. Turn the ends in, take the tape over to the right side of the fabric and pin the folded edge to the machine stitched line. Stitch the edge of the bias tape to the right side by hand with ladder stitch. Repeat for the other triangle. On the inside piece of fabric, press the turning allowance back to make a 15 in. square. Turn the raw edges under to make a hem, pin in place and machine stitch along the folded edges.

5. To make the blue tie, take the remainder of the bias tape, fold it in half lengthwise and stitch down both sides by machine. Cut this length in half and tie a knot in one end of each half. Fold the other end back under itself to make a loop and pin it to the right side of the triangle's point. Oversew the tape by hand, making sure the end is anchored securely. Make the white ties by folding the bias tape back on itself widthwise and stitching to make a wider tie. First cut the remaining tape length in two for each tie. Fold one back on itself widthwise and pin the wrong sides together. Stitch by machine, starting at the raw ends. Stitch down one side, across the folded end and up the other side. Stitch onto the cushion by folding the raw end under, then pinning to the right side of the point and machine stitching in a square.

6. Slip the cushion into and between the layers and tie a bow on the front. The blue ties make a string bow and the white ties make a flat bow.

Octagonal Windows

■●■●■●■●■●■●■●■●■●■●■●■●■●■●■●■●■

THE INSPIRATION FOR THIS QUILT WAS THE BEAUTIFUL, LATTICED WINDOWS SEEN IN INDIA AND MIDDLE EASTERN COUNTRIES. THESE WINDOWS MAKE CHANGING SHADOWS INDOORS AS THE SUN MOVES AROUND DURING THE DAY. LOOKING THROUGH THEM, YOU CAN OFTEN SEE A GARDEN THAT HAS BEEN BROKEN INTO GEOMETRIC SHAPES FRAMED BY THE LATTICEWORK.

FINISHED QUILT SIZE: 122 INCHES SQUARE (KING SIZED)

YOU WILL NEED

Materials

◆ stone colored cotton, 11½ yd × 45 in.

◆ printed cotton, 81 pieces of scraps of 20 × 20 in. or fat quarters

◆ cotton flannel sheet, one king sized sheet

Pattern Guides

(Measurements for the octagons are given at their widest points.)

● A 21 in. octagon

● B 16 in. octagon

● C 13 in. octagon

● D 12 in. octagon

● E 10 in. square

● F   8 in. square

● G   7 in. square

Number of pieces to cut

■ A 40 × stone colored cotton octagons

■ B 40 × cotton flannel octagons

■ C 40 × printed cotton octagons

■ E 41 × printed cotton squares

■ F 41 × cotton flannel squares and 41 × stone colored cotton squares

1. The octagons are folded like the hexagons, by placing pattern B on the wrong side of the fabric, folding the turnings back and pressing. Remove the paper, insert the padding and baste the pieces together.

2. For the smaller octagons repeat the above process, using pattern D but, before removing the paper, baste the folded corners in place with backstitch in the folds only. Remove the paper and turn right side up onto the center of the large octagon. Matching the points to the folds, pin in place and quilt around the edges.

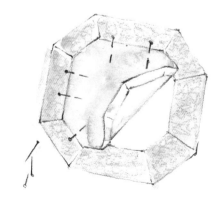

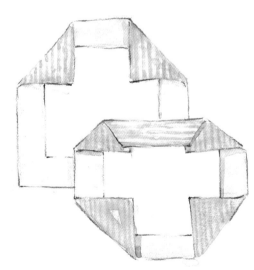

3. Fold the squares following the instructions in Basic Techniques, pp.8–9 for squares folded into squares. Quilt around the edges to hold the pieces together.

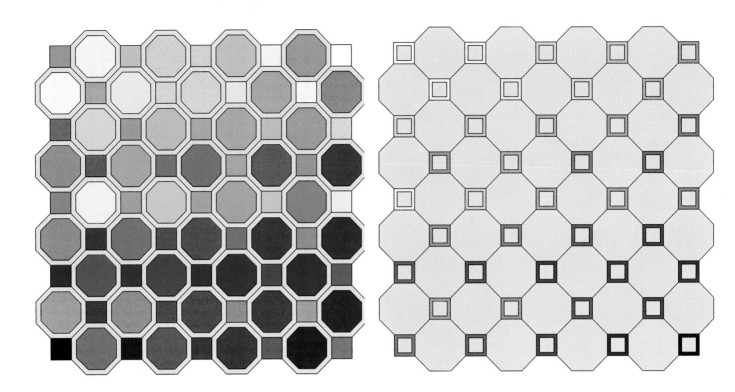

Octagonal Windows color charts
front (left), back (right)

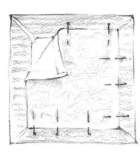

4. Lay out all the pieces with the octagons right side up and the squares face down. Arrange the pieces according to the colors and shades from dark to light, or scatter the pieces for a random effect. If you have never done this before, invite a friend to do it with you, to move the pieces and see the whole thing with another pair of eyes. Another helpful hint is to do the layout on a full-sized sheet of fabric, so that when the placement is finally decided the pieces can be pinned to it with safety pins.

5. When the order of the pieces is decided, lift the sheet, and fold it in rows across the width. Ladder stitch the pieces together in rows of octagons and squares. When you have two rows, join these across the whole width, thus building the quilt up to the full size.

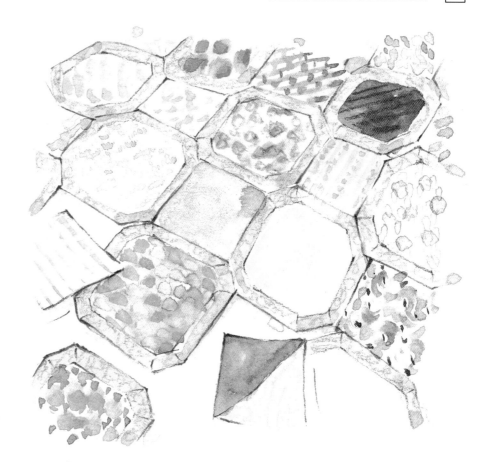

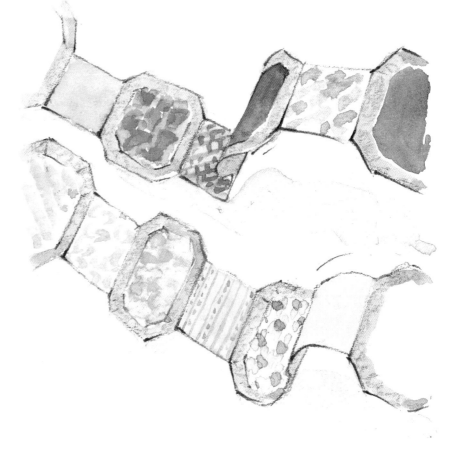

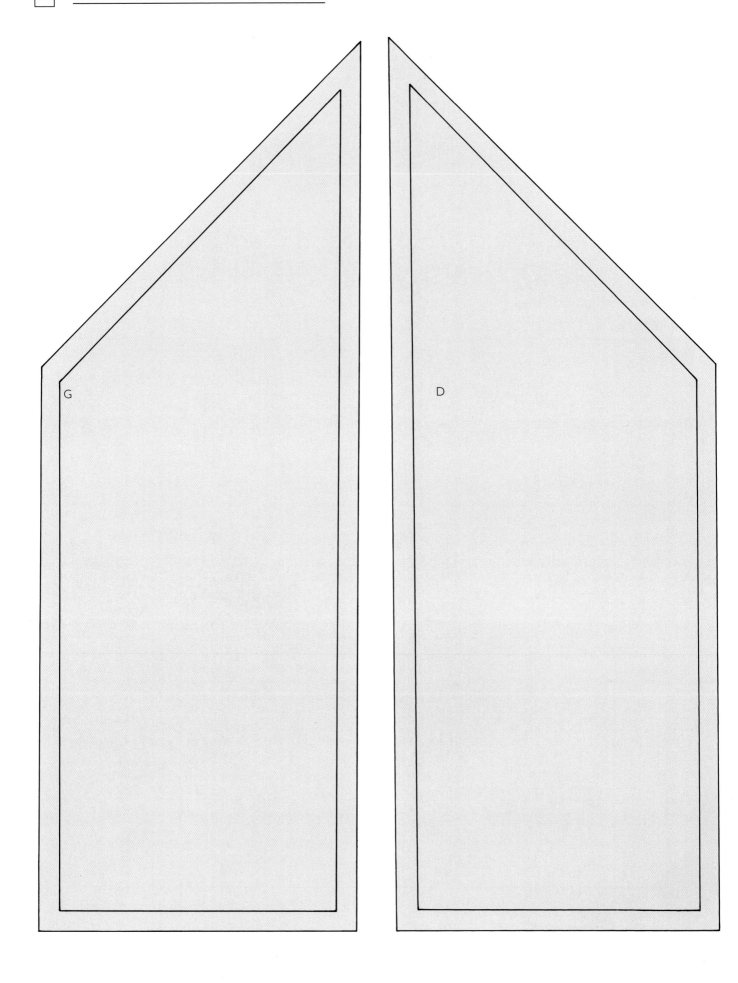

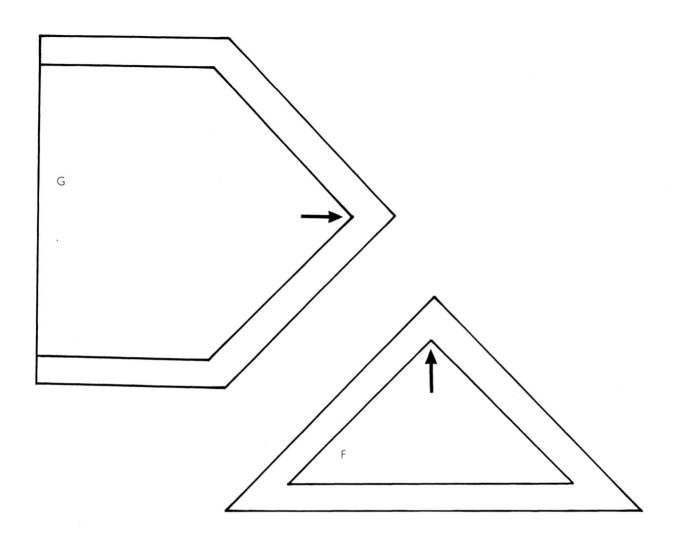

G

F

VICTORIAN TILES : actual size

VICTORIAN TILES : actual size

E

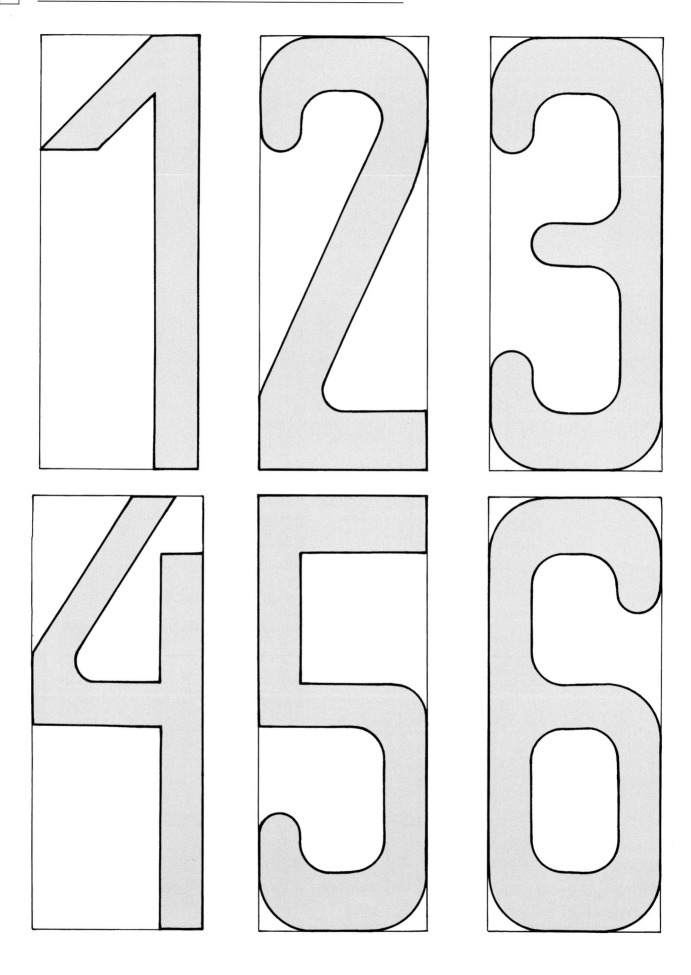

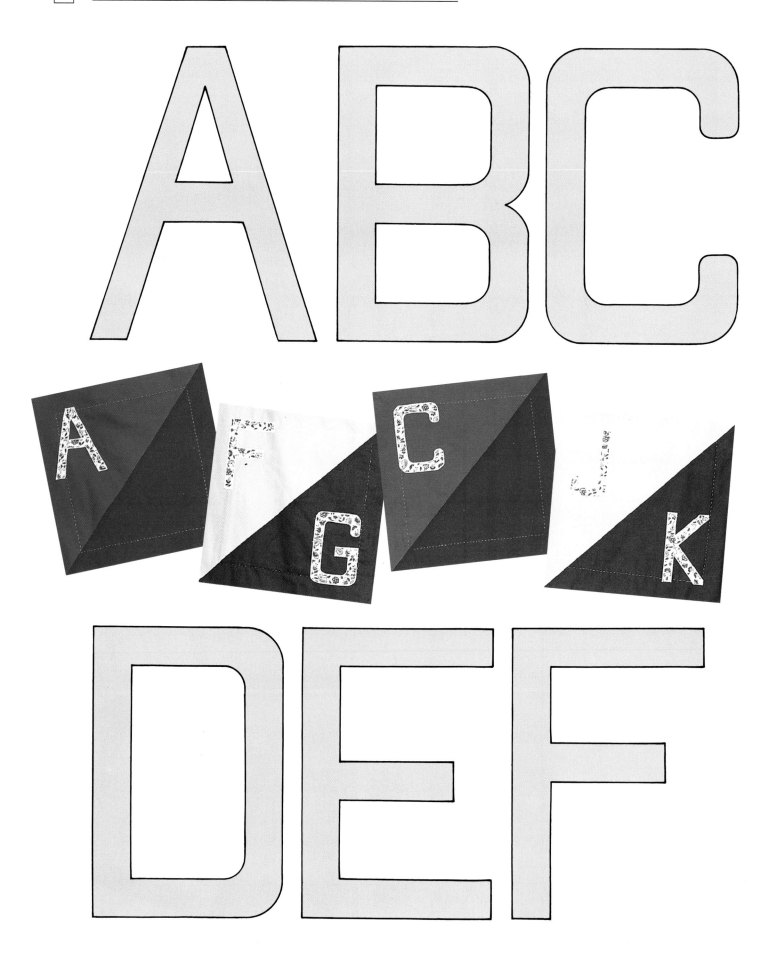

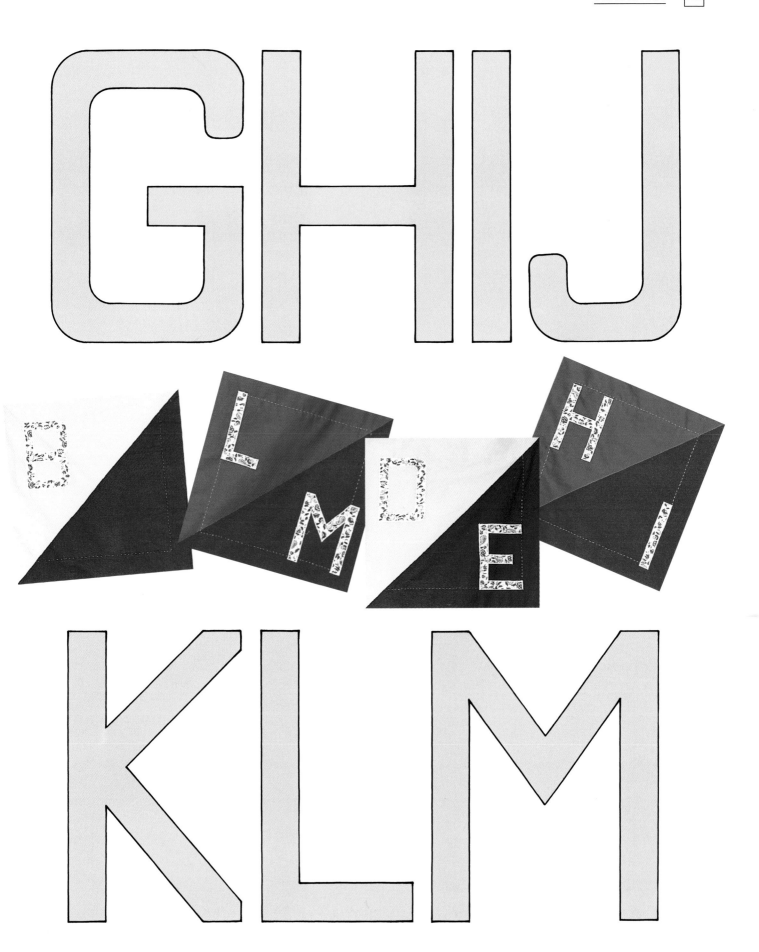

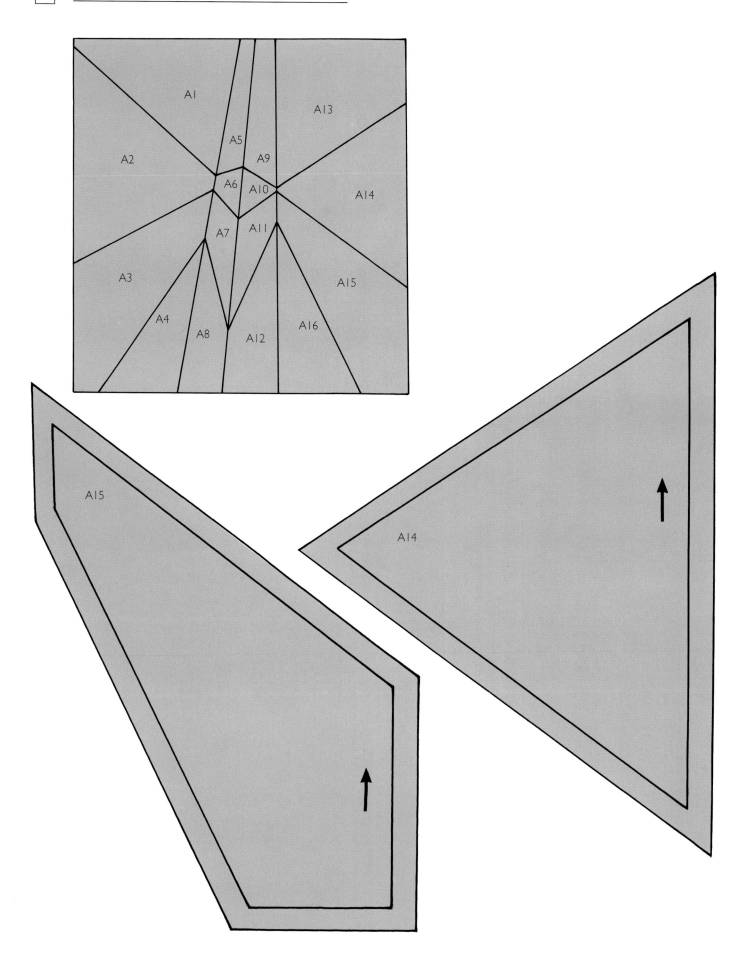

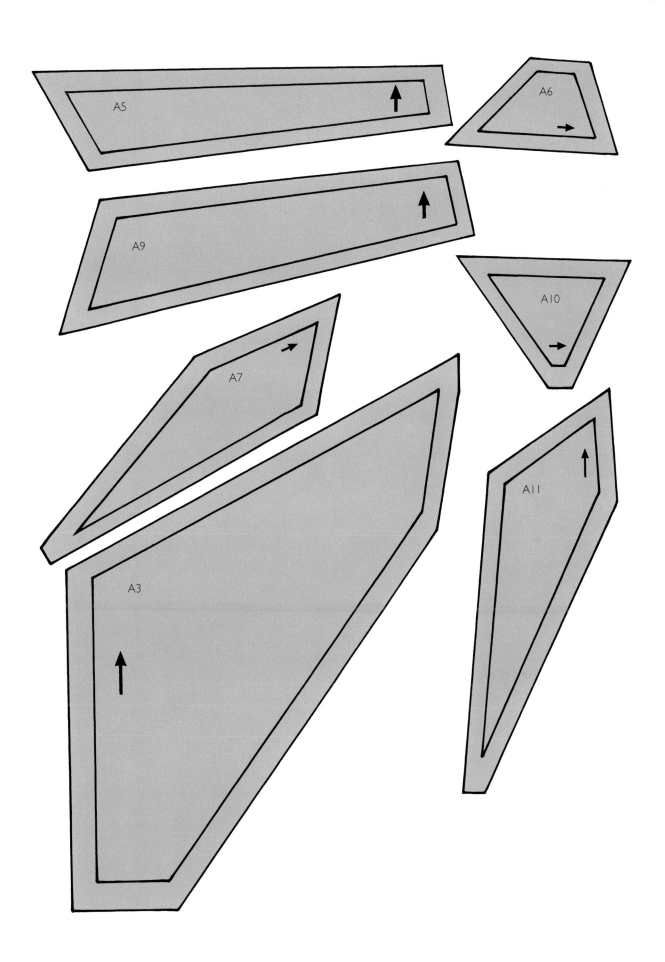

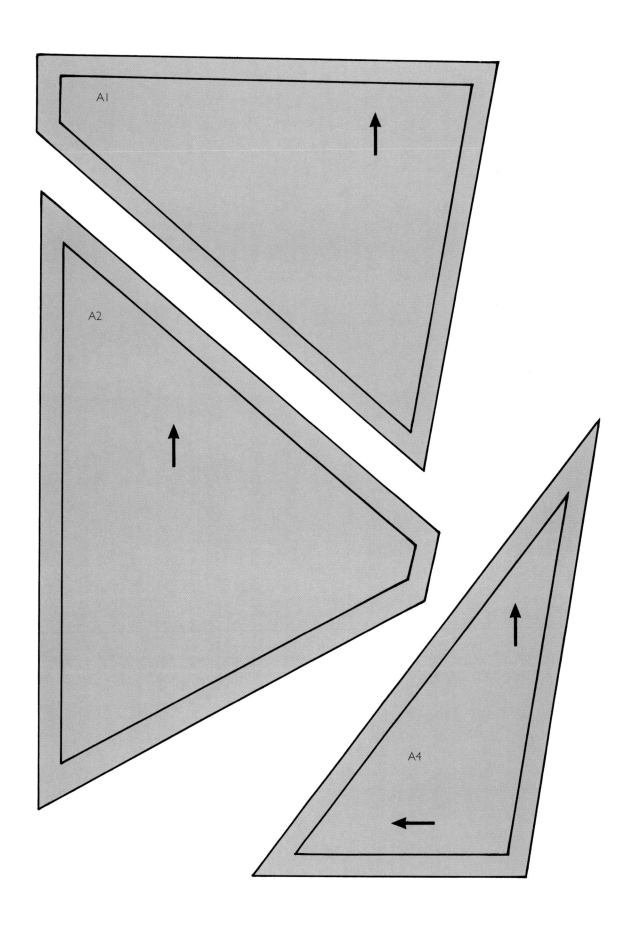

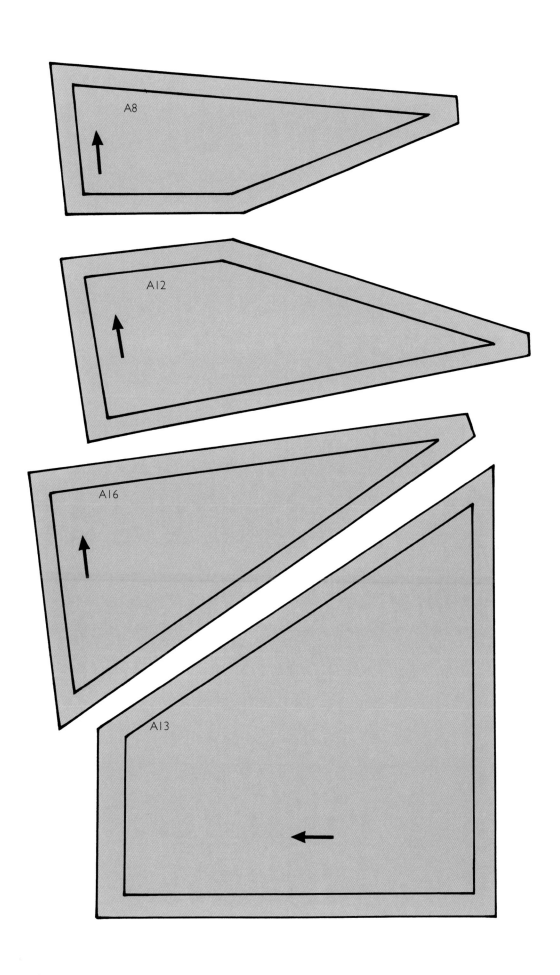

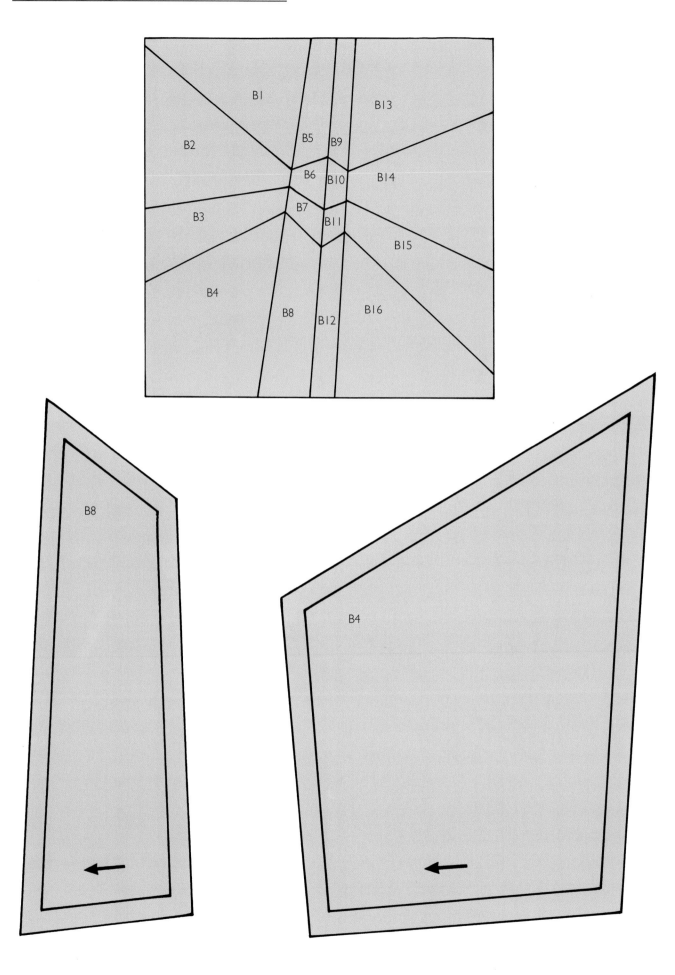

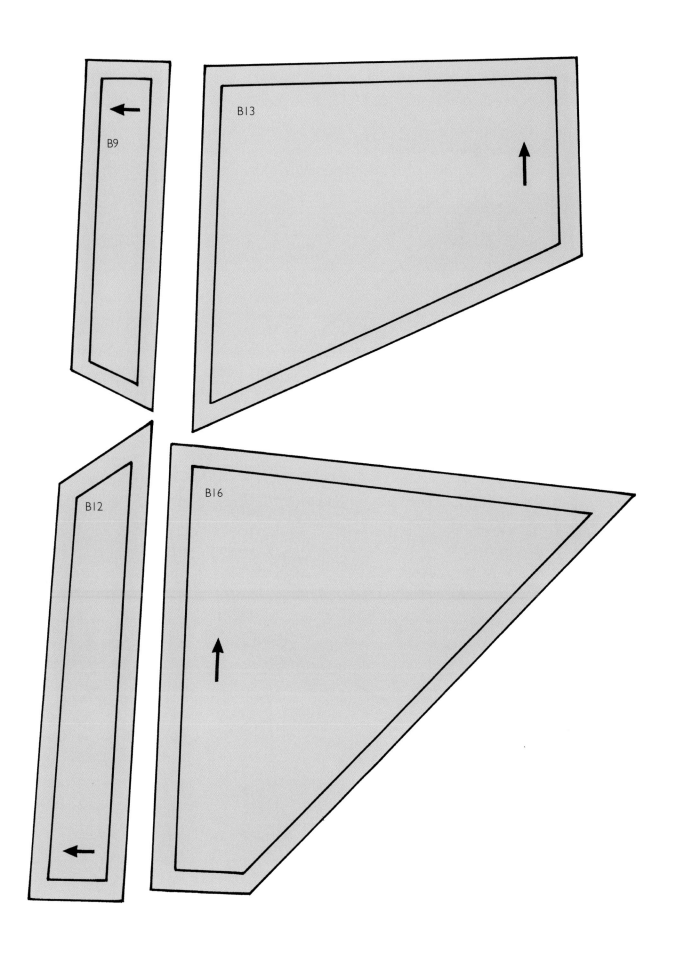

B9

B13

B12

B16

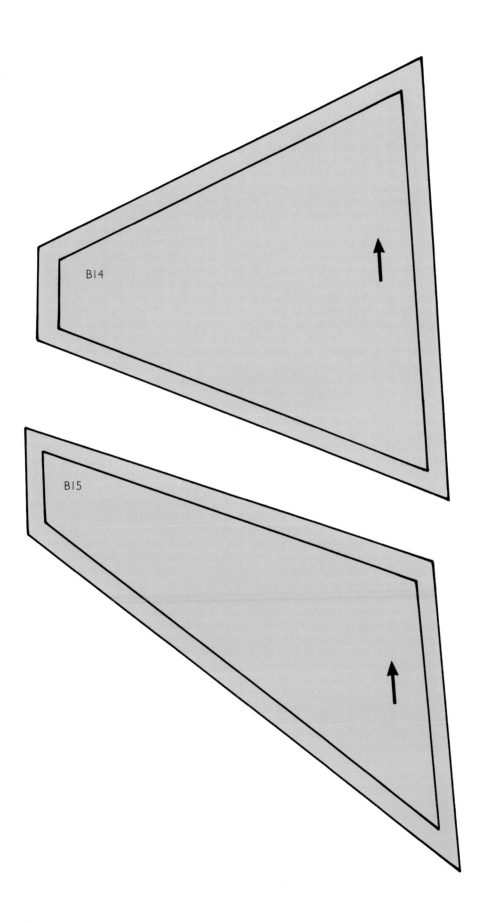

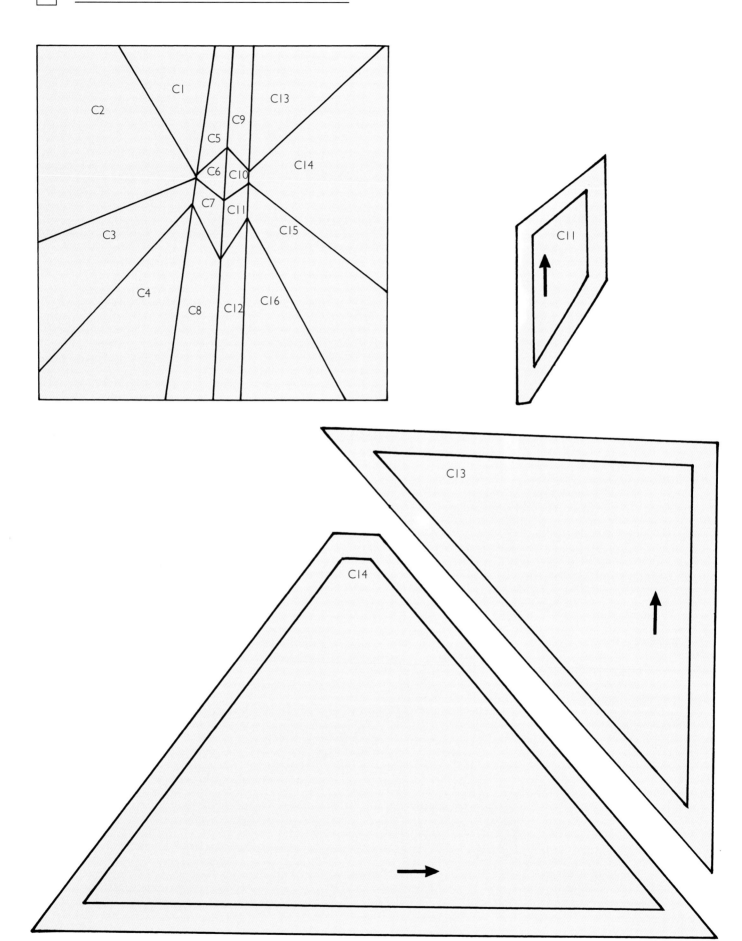

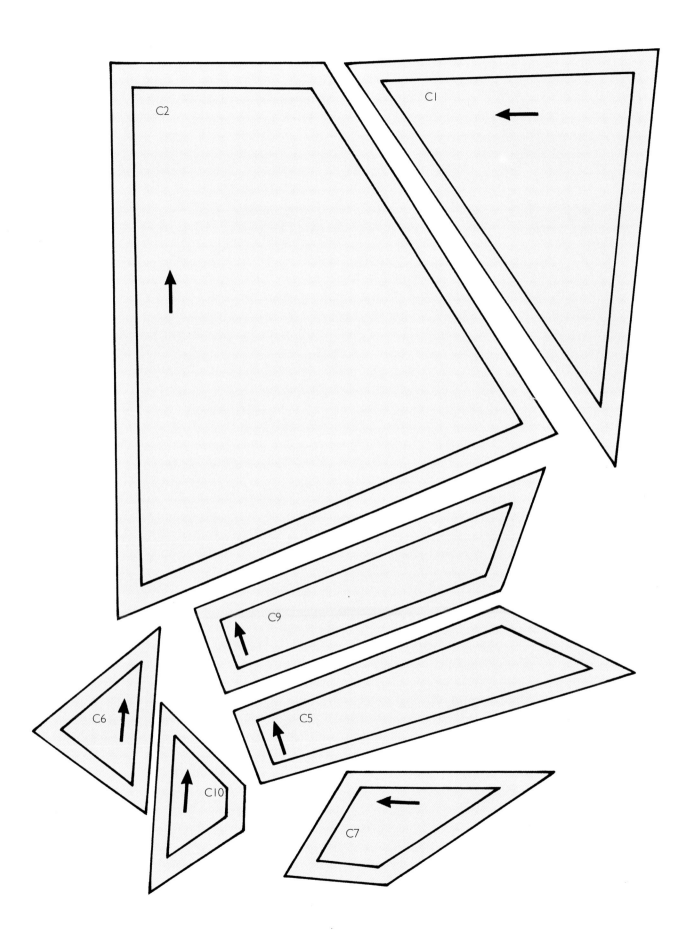

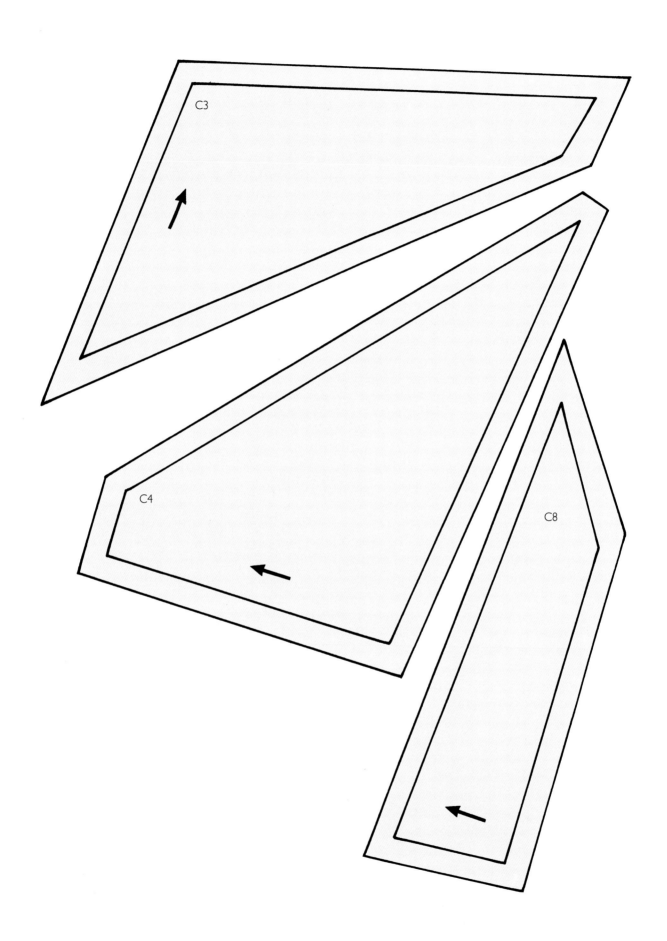

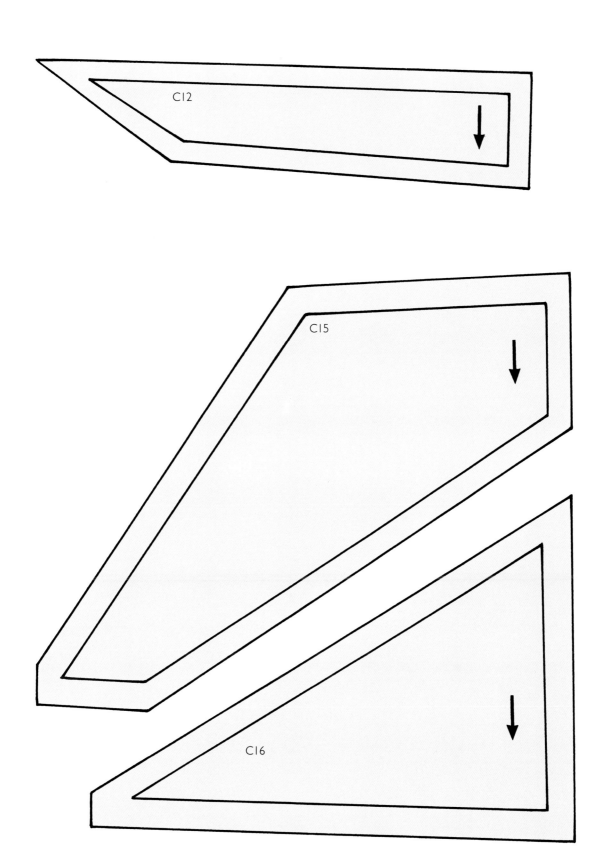

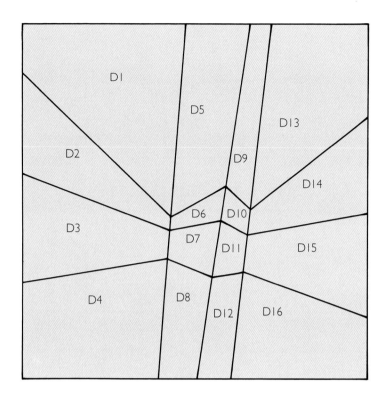

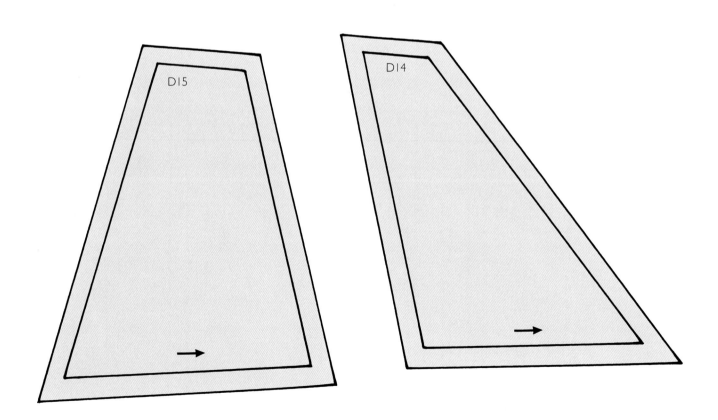

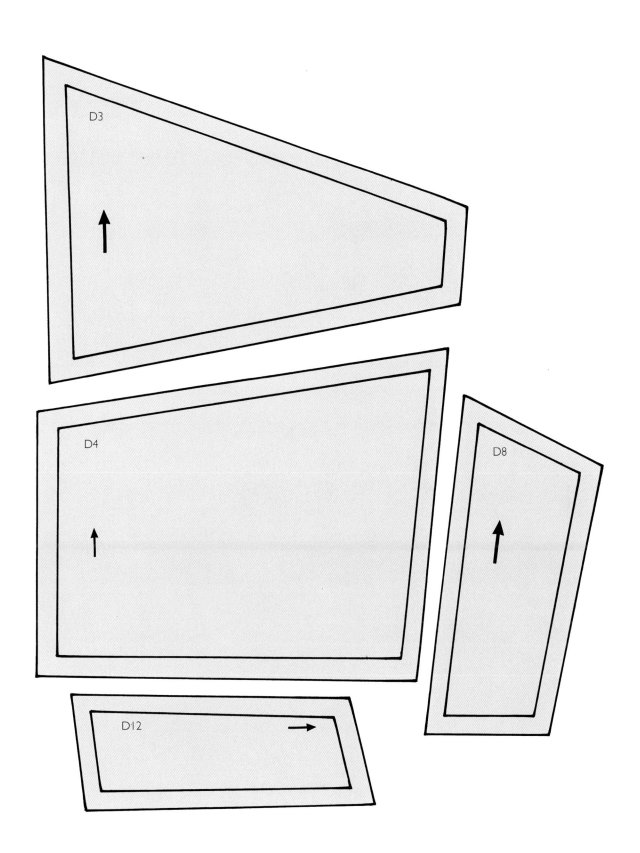

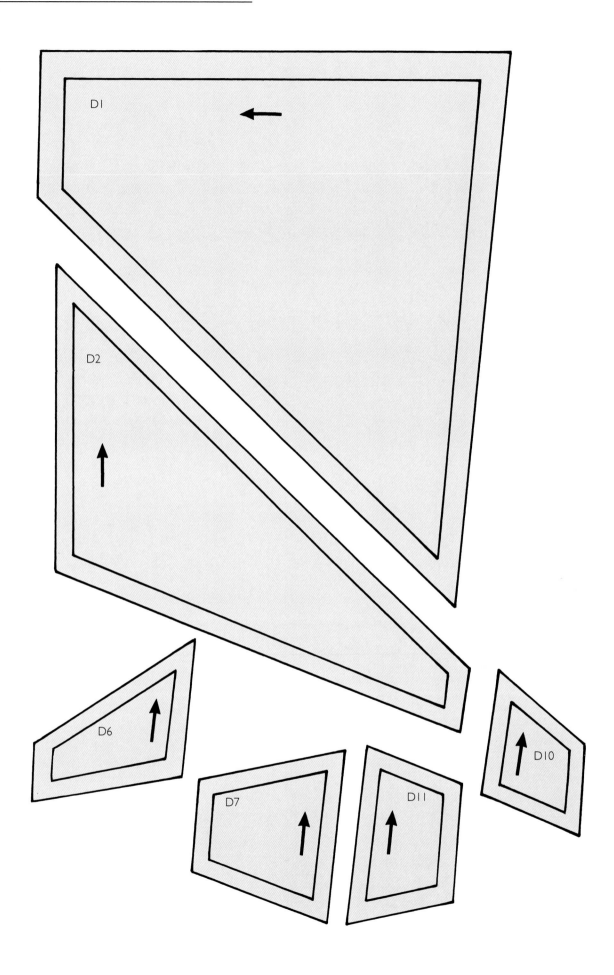

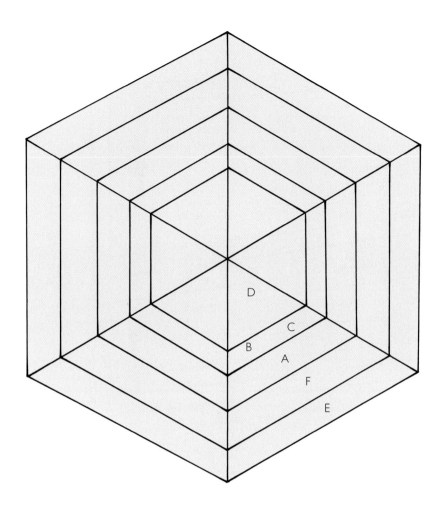

HEXAGON BAG PP85-87
50% actual size

GREEN FLOWER THROWOVER PP77-81
actual size

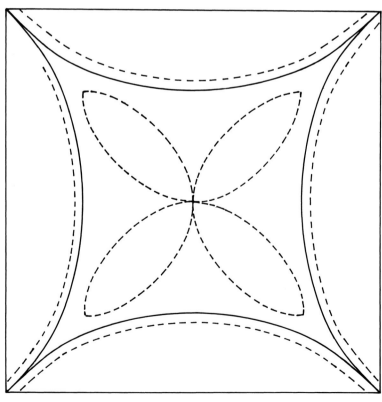

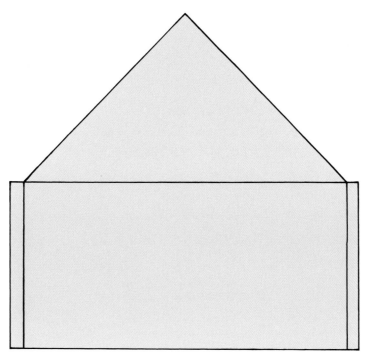

INDIAN CUSHION COVERS pp.92-95
25% actual size

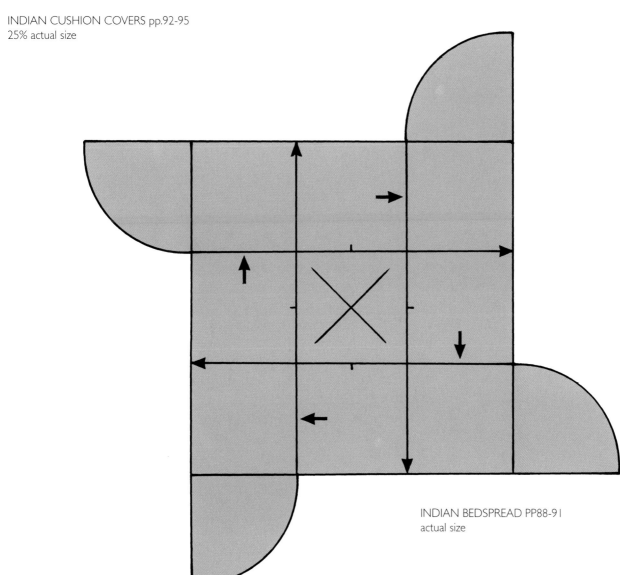

INDIAN BEDSPREAD PP88-91
actual size

Index